A Butler's Guide to
Gentlemen's
Grooming

A Butler's Guide to
Gentlemen's
Grooming

Nicholas Clayton

BATSFORD

This edition published in 2016 by
Batsford, an imprint of Pavilion Books Group Ltd
1 Gower St
London WC1E 6HD

First published in the United Kingdom in 2010 by National Trust Books

ISBN: 9781849943703

A CIP catalogue record for this book is available from the British Library.

20 19 18 17 16
10 9 8 7 6 5 4 3 2 1

Reproduction by Mission Productions, Hong Kong
Printed by Toppan Leefung Printing Ltd, China

This book can be ordered direct from the publisher at the website:
www.pavilionbooks.com, or try your local bookshop.

For JD

CONTENTS

INTRODUCTION 8

HAIR TODAY, GONE TOMORROW 14

SQUEAKY CLEAN 26

SWEATING 34

A CLOSE SHAVE 40

WORD OF MOUTH 52

SKIN-CARE ESSENTIALS 62

DIET AND WELL BEING 72

HOW TO DRESS: THE ART OF
LOOKING GOOD   78

DEPORTMENT   94

BE YOUR OWN VALET   100

WATCH YOUR STEP   120

SWAG   132

DRESS CODES   138

APPENDIX   156

INDEX   160

INTRODUCTION

England alas, my country! Has degenerated very much, and is degenerating every day. She has not many gentlemen left. We are few. I see nothing to succeed us but a race of weavers.

Mr Turveydrop in *Bleak House* by Charles Dickens

Years ago, when I started to lose my hair, I was a bit concerned. After all no one likes going bald; perhaps it's a fear of having to accept that the inevitable ageing process is starting to show or perhaps a concern about being called names such as 'baldy'.

Every time I went for a haircut my barber suggested that I should have it all shaved off. I eventually gave in and had what remained of my thinning hair cut off. It is a style that is very easy to look after and is actually quite rejuvenating. I'm sure I look younger every time I go in for a 'number two-and-a-half', which must be a good thing. Another useful aspect of having my hair cut short is that I haven't needed to comb my hair for nearly twelve years! My barber says that, rather than lament the passing of the thatch, one should just wear whatever one has with pride.

Pride in oneself is very important and – in exactly the same way that holding a knife and fork incorrectly will betray you and in one mouthful reveal your lack of training – so sloppy, slovenly attention to personal grooming will do exactly the same thing. Clean hair, teeth and fingernails are in our society the very basic of basic requirements in terms of personal hygiene, things that are extremely easy to achieve and to maintain.

Again to draw on the table manners analogy, who wants to sit at a table with someone with disgusting table manners? We all know, or should know by now, that eating like a pig is one of the quickest ways of being discounted for promotion, missing out on a date or simply not being asked back.

Likewise then, who wants to be seen with a scruffy, dirty individual with unkempt, filthy hair and fingernails, foul breath and stinking armpits? And furthermore, who wants to be that dirty individual?

To a certain extent the whole personal hygiene question is seen by some as a difficult one to discuss and a difficult one to broach – even a 'taboo' subject. How do you tell someone, for example, that they smell of sweaty armpits or that they have offensive breath? Well, as a butler I don't have a problem with this. If I had staff around me that needed to bath or change their shirt or use a stronger mouthwash, believe me, I would tell them. In fact, only very recently I had to remind someone that using a deodorant and a toothbrush is generally accepted as a good idea.

If personal hygiene was not considered such an important subject, the shelves of supermarkets and chemists would not be stacked to the ceilings with washing, shampooing and cosmetic products, and shops and departments stores wouldn't sell shirts. The market for these products in the UK alone accounts for millions of pounds in sales revenue annually. Clearly the products are important and millions of people are already up to speed, but it seems to me that there are also plenty who are not.

Looking good and being washed, shaved and well groomed is a vital part of our everyday lives. It shows pride in ourselves, is healthy and gives us confidence – that should be the goal. As well as washing and dressing like a gentleman, so behaving like one and knowing how to behave in company is just as important if you want to send the right message and give the right impression; deportment too plays a role, indeed it is every bit as vital as a clean shirt. This guide is designed to help everyone achieve that goal.

Nicholas Clayton

HAIR TODAY, GONE TOMORROW

L ooking after your hair is an essential part of being well groomed, but there are a few basic rules to follow if you want to keep hair healthy and looking good.

Keeping hair healthy

A single strand of hair is made up of about 25 per cent water, so drinking plenty of water has to be a good way to maintain supple hair. Iron helps to carry oxygen to the hair, and without enough iron the hair and the follicles become starved of oxygen. Zinc builds hair protein, which can help towards slowing down hair loss. Pigmentation is influenced by copper levels and it is possible to optimise your natural shade with a diet high in copper. Vitamins B and C help with circulation, good hair growth and colour, and vitamin A will give you a healthy scalp.

The best advice is to avoid chemicals on your hair, such as chlorine from swimming pools and even sea water. Wet the hair or apply a conditioner before going swimming, or shower off the water from the pool or the sea as soon as possible after getting out. Physical wear from everyday friction is to blame for most hair damage; even friction from a pillowcase can cause breakage. Avoid blow drying because the intense heat is detrimental to the hair and the scalp, as is brushing the hair when it is wet, because wet hair is weaker than dry hair.

Massage the scalp after washing the hair to increase blood-flow and rinse with cold water after showering to close the follicles, thus lessening the chance of damage.

Don't wash your hair every day unless you have an especially oily scalp; shampooing two to three times a week should be sufficient to remove dirt and build-up. Some permanent or semi-permanent colours can be harmful to hair, so consider staying your natural colour.

Alopecia

The correct term for hair loss is alopecia and the most common type is known as androgenetic alopecia, or male pattern baldness.

Going bald is a fact of life for millions of men. It is not inevitable that a man goes bald. In fact, in about 95 per cent of cases, male hair loss from the head is due to genetic inheritance. Hair lives for around five years and most adults lose about a hundred scalp hairs every day. In the case of the balding man these lost hairs do not necessarily get replaced and the thinning starts to become apparent, but the process can take a long time.

Unfortunately most men are genetically predisposed to male pattern baldness. It is the effect of hormones on the hair follicle that produces the bald patches. Testosterone, a hormone that is present in high levels in men after puberty, is converted to dihydrotestosterone. This has an adverse affect on hair follicles, slowing down hair production and producing weak, shorter hair. Sometimes it stops hair growth from the follicle completely.

When my hair fell out in clumps following a period of stress, my doctor told me that it might grow back and, if and when it did, it would more than likely be white. My hair did grow back white – I looked like a badger for about six months, after which it all miraculously returned to its former dreary brown.

The Norwood-Hamilton scale diagram (shown opposite) helps to pinpoint the stage of hair loss you may be at. As the name male 'pattern' baldness suggests, the thinning gradually follows a pattern. When men in their twenties to forties start to lose their hair, the chances are that it is male pattern baldness. The pattern generally starts at the temples and/or the front of the hairline.

There are drugs on the market that are said to help in a restorative way, but the proof is scanty. You could attempt to disguise the fact that you are balding by cultivating a 'comb-over', where the hair is grown incredibly long above one ear, then combed over the top of the head. This will only work until the wind dislodges it. Alternatively, you could have the remaining hair cut very short, which is rejuvenating and cheap in terms of shampoo usage.

The best way to wash the balding scalp is with a mild shampoo and a conditioner and then, if you want to, massage some moisturiser into the bald area as well.

Norwood-Hamilton scale for male pattern baldness

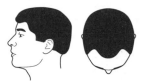

Stage 1: Full head of hair.

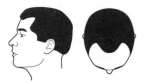

Stage 2: Small amount of loss at the hairline.

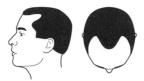

Stage 3: Visible loss at the hairline.

Stage 4: Increased loss at the hairline and at the crown.

Stage 5: Hair loss extends to the vertex.

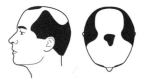

Stage 6: Areas of hair loss at the hairline and vertex merge.

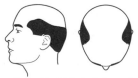

Stage 7: All hair is lost along the front hairline and crown.

Dealing with greasy hair

Environmental dirt and bacteria can add to the problem of greasy or oily hair. Greasy hair is caused by oil secreted by the sebaceous glands in the skin; it makes the hair unmanageable and it can look unpleasant and smell dirty.

and some more hints on dealing with greasy hair...

- Wash greasy hair more frequently and not in water that is too hot.
- Don't scrub and rub like mad; it only goes to further activate sebaceous glands that are already over-activated.
- Cut down on the use of conditioners, to about once every two weeks.
- Reduce your intake of fatty food. Quite apart from the fact that we all know over-indulgence is not good for us, fatty foods will increase the likelihood of the hair becoming greasy. If you have seen the film *Super Size Me* you will know what fatty food can do to your heart in only a very short time – imagine what it could also be doing to your hair.
- Buy and use a shampoo that is specifically designed for greasy hair.
- Try some lemon juice in the final rinse for a healthy shine.

Dealing with dry hair

Dry hair is for some people a natural phenomenon, or it can be caused by heat and the elements. The tips of the hair are most at risk, as they are not in direct contact with the scalp and can't utilise the sebum oil the scalp produces.

If your hair is really dry, try massaging an oil (such as coconut oil) into the hair. Take one or two drops of the oil in your hands and rub together, but do not use too much; there should only be enough to make your hands shiny. Rub the oil into dry hair, only the ends at first then the middle section of the hair. Leave the oil in your hair.

and some more hints on dealing with dry hair...

- Don't wash your hair every day. Shampooing two or three times a week should be enough to remove dirt and product build-up.
- Buy and use a shampoo that is specifically designed for dry hair.
- Use shampoos and conditioners that contain humectants. These are ingredients, such as glycerine, which help bind water to the hair to reduce dryness; they replace lost moisture and attract more moisture, which they retain in the cortex of the hair.

Dandruff

Dandruff is a common problem and affects most people at some time during their life. Dandruff consists of pieces of dead skin cells that fall away from the scalp. The entire body discards dead skin cells all the time and every 24–28 days we produce completely new skin. Dandruff and, for that matter, other skin ailments, such as psoriasis, are a result of the skin regenerating at a much faster rate than normal. Sometimes the rate at which the skin cells depart the surface of the skin is so fast that they are not even dead. In some people, the occurrence of dandruff is very visible, especially on the collar area.

Because skin regeneration is a natural process there is no official cure for dandruff, but there are a few ways to help control the causes. Most over-the-counter dandruff-specific shampoos attack the fungus known as *Pityrosporum ovale*, which is thought to be a major cause of the problem. Dandruff often leaves the scalp feeling very itchy and sensitive, so use products that contain chemicals with care. The apparently efficacious ingredients to look out for include climbazole, zinc pyrithione, octopirox and ketoconazole. Massage the dandruff-eliminating shampoo into the scalp gently to help exfoliate the dead cells and rinse very well.

Some possible causes of dandruff include poor health or hygiene, hormonal imbalance, allergic hypersensitivity, tiredness, stress or anxiety, bad nutrition, including too much sugar, starch and fat in your diet, over-usage of hair-styling products, infrequent shampooing or inadequate rinsing, over-heating with hairdryers, cold weather and dry indoor heating.

In common with other ailments, if the problem is particularly excessive, consult your doctor.

Colouring your hair

There all sorts of reasons why you may decide to dye your hair – just for a change, for a fancy dress party, to cover up the grey or, perhaps, you need to escape the law. It can be as dramatic or as subtle a change to your look as you wish. If you want to achieve a natural look rather than simply dyeing it green at home, it's probably best to have it done by a professional stylist. Not everyone's skin can cope with the chemicals involved in the chameleonic exercise so it's definitely worthwhile having a skin test before the specialist dons the rubber gloves; hydrogen peroxide, the chemical used in hair dyes, is very strong.

Choosing a hair colour

Choose a colour to complement your skin tone.
Light-skinned people don't often suit very dark
hair because it draws colour out of their skin.

If you want to go blond, this needs to be done with
a permanent dye, and is a relatively simple job for a
trained stylist. Tanned skin can look very unnatural
when mixed with a one-tone blond.

Brunette colours suit most people and varying the shades
can achieve a large range of looks from chocolate browns
and bronzes to honey or dark blonde. Some really rich
chestnut colours can look artificial and obviously dyed.

Black is the easiest colour to get right. It looks best
on people with darker and olive skin tones.

Colouring grey hair

If your hair doesn't fall out, sooner or later it will
probably go grey; it happens to everyone. If grey
hair is a bit too natural for you, you can tone it
down, blend it in or cover it up using hair dye.

If your hair is more than half to completely grey, you'll need a permanent process to dye it. Try to resist the temptation to go darker than your natural colour and pick a shade as close to your natural colour as possible. This will make your regrowth roots less obvious.

If your hair is less than half grey, you can probably use a strong semi-permanent process or stick with a longer-lasting permanent. Be mindful that grey and white hair is often more resistant to colour, so leave the dye on for the maximum amount of time. Always try a strand test first.

If you are only slightly grey, gentle semi-permanents and temporary colours are good choices; they are easy to apply at home. Pick one that is close to your natural colour and the grey will turn to highlights. If you've decided to let nature take its course but still want a little help, temporary colours can make the white and grey less of a contrast by increasing the 'pepper' component of salt-and-pepper hair.

SQUEAKY CLEAN

OLFACTORY FACTS

olfactory (olfacteRi) *adj*. pertaining to the sense
of smell.
stink (stink) *v*. emit strongly unpleasant smell,
be highly offensive.
stinker (stinker) *n*. one who or that which has
an offensive smell, very unpleasant person.
The Concise Oxford Dictionary, 9th edition

The medical and scientific jury seems to be out when it
comes to explaining exactly how we smell. The olfactory
process is a complicated one to understand. Put very
simply, every odour is made up of molecules, although
we can't see them, and these molecules have a particular
shape. Receptors in the olfactory nerve determine the
type of odour, depending on how the molecule fits into
the receptor, which is how we detect unpleasant smells.
A clever system; one that is more than likely set up to
warn us of things that are potentially dangerous for the
human body. Well, you wouldn't eat a rotting apple
would you? At least, you wouldn't if you smelled
it first.

The human body does smell and, left unwashed for
any length of time, can smell very unpleasant. Bearing
in mind the olfactory system described above, it would
seem obvious that if we find a bodily smell unpleasant it
is probably not very healthy and therefore clearly not
good for us to ignore it.

It's a plain enough fact that, if we smell, it is not very nice and certainly not very polite to subject those around us to the odours emitted by our unwashed body.

There is, for example, absolutely nothing worse than being around someone with unwashed armpits, or sitting next to a person who really ought to change their underwear, producing smells we find totally abhorrent. Although there are some medical reasons why some people suffer with body odour, most people agree that it is not socially acceptable to smell and most of us would be embarrassed to think that this was the case. The simple answer is to wash and to wear clean clothes. A bar of soap and a deodorant is relatively inexpensive, so there is no excuse whatsoever.

Bathing or showering

Apart from the amount of water a bath takes as opposed to the smaller amount used by showering, the choice whether to use a bath or a shower is a personal thing and each has its own benefits. Bathing is a great way to relax but is not ideal if the body is heavily soiled after outdoor activities, for example, where it would be more prudent to wash the dirt off quickly with a shower.

Washing with products that are as chemical free as possible is the first step to healthy skin.

Skin and healthcare professionals in the UK recommend that the face, underarms and undercarriage are washed at least once a day. Any more than this and evidence suggests that naturally occurring essential oils that are beneficial to the skin will be washed away. Nevertheless, many people prefer to bathe once in the morning and again before going to bed.

Now wash your hands

It would seem obvious to me that you should wash your hands as often as possible. Hands come into constant contact with bacteria. Certainly if you are working with food (cooking or preparing), keeping your hands clean is a basic requirement and it should be a matter of course to wash them frequently. Wash your hands before you come to the dinner table and, most importantly, wash your hands after you have been to the lavatory. If there is one, use a paper towel to open the door of a public lavatory on your way out after you have washed your hands – there is absolutely no telling what might be on the door handle.

If you blow your nose or sneeze into your hands go and wash them immediately; not doing so is impolite and can spread germs. If you smoke, wash your hands after you have put the cigarette out otherwise your hands will stink!

It may be an urban myth, and certainly I can't find any scientific tests to prove it, but we have all heard about how much urine from unwashed fingers can be found in a bowl of peanuts on a pub bar. Regardless of whether this myth is true or not, you should never put your hands in your mouth – can you imagine how much bacteria there is on a banknote or coin?

Avoid sandwich shops or the cold meat counters where the operative is wearing gloves. It's a curious thing to watch; they seem to think that it's acceptable to straighten their hair, pick at their nose and take your money if they have gloves on. In fact, all they are doing is protecting their own hands and passing on the germs.

Drying

All persons should have their own towel to dry themselves and, ideally, it should be washed after each use. Bacteria and infections can multiply very quickly on a damp towel.

Skin should be patted dry, so that the skin retains a small amount of moisture. Don't rub too vigorously as this can lead to over dry skin and irritation. Dry all areas well and pay particular attention to the spaces between the toes. Leaving these places damp can lead to irritating infections such as athlete's foot.

Sorry, what did you say?

Wash inside your ears; having dirty ears with wax visible from the outside is really not acceptable. Clean the outer parts of the ear with a cotton bud but be very careful not to delve too deeply because you can damage the ear. A build-up of ear wax is a removal job for your doctor and in extreme cases, if the amount is large enough, can lead to hearing loss.

Fingernails

Clean fingernails are an essential part of the grooming procedure. Dirty, unkempt fingernails are a big turn-off on a man, as are long nails! Start by buying a finger nailbrush, which are cheap and available from every supermarket or chemist. The best way to clean your nails is to use the fingernail brush either before or immediately after a shower or bath. Use the specially designed end of a nail file to clean the dirt out from under the nail, but be careful not to dig too far.

Weekly trimming of nails with scissors or clippers is generally sufficient. They should never be longer than 3mm (⅛ in) in length. Trim the ends of the nails and part of the sides and then shape them with a file or emery board, filing in one direction. Cuticles are the fine layer of skin that protrudes above the nail surface and, as the nail grows, can become dry and ragged. Cuticles should be gently pushed back in the direction of the first finger joint. Extend this regime to your toenails.

Fingernail biting is very unpleasant. Quite apart from the fact that you will swallow all the dirt that is under the nail, bitten nails look awful. If you really can't stop, there are some very nasty-tasting products that you can use to paint on the nails that are so ghastly you will definitely lose the urge to nibble.

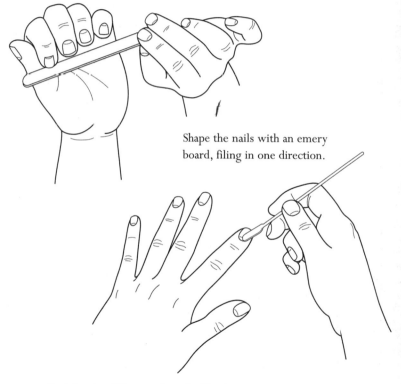

Shape the nails with an emery board, filing in one direction.

Cuticles should be gently pushed back in the direction of the first finger joint.

SWEATING

The average person has approximately 2.6 million sweat glands. They are distributed over the whole body except for the lips, the nipples and our external genital areas. Also called perspiration, sweat is produced as a way for the body to cool itself.

There are two types of sweat glands: eccrine and apocrine. Eccrine glands are active from birth. They are found all over the body, including the palms of the hands, the soles of the feet and the forehead. They are smaller than apocrine glands and produce sweat that is free from proteins and fatty acids. Apocrine glands become active at puberty. They are slightly larger, mostly confined to the armpits and the genital area, and typically end in hair follicles. They produce sweat that contains fatty acids and proteins. In the ears there are modified apocrine glands called ceruminous glands that are responsible for the production of ear wax.

We sweat after exercise, during moments of emotional stress and if the air temperature around us is high. When the water in our sweat evaporates it leaves behind salts such as sodium chloride and potassium. It is possible for the average man to lose 1–1.5 litres (1¾–2½ pints) of liquid through sweating every day. Do some exercise and it is possible to lose up to 3 litres (5¼ pints) in an hour.

Combating sweat

Soap and water is the best remedy for sweating – use an anti-bacterial soap if you want to. It is a good idea to use an anti-perspirant or a deodorant under the arms after washing. Most standard deodorant and anti-perspirant products can contain some fairly hefty amounts of chemicals – it is widely known that aluminium will block perspiration – so choose carefully.

Shaving the hair off under the arms has long been part of most women's grooming regime. There is nothing wrong with men doing the same or, alternatively, just cut hair back with scissors and leave a small amount visible to retain a masculine look. The fact is that this simple procedure significantly reduces the risk of smelly armpits – applying a deodorant other than a spray is quite difficult and very wasteful when there is a carpet of hair in the way. Do not apply any deodorants or anti-perspirants to cut or damaged skin.

An unscented product is best or one that matches your eau de toilette or aftershave. All fragrances should be kept discreet as there is a risk that one fragrance could clash with the other – even though, according to advertising, some products will have hordes of women following you.

If you have been sweating excessively during exercise or for any other reason, drink plenty of fluids to replace the loss. The loss of salt and fluid can dehydrate you very quickly.

There are many causes of excessive sweating and one could be hyperhidrosis. If you are in any doubt or you think you are sweating too much, see your doctor.

Sweaty feet

Feet are among the most sweaty parts of the body due to an estimated 250,000 sweat glands per foot, which is a higher concentration of sweat glands per square inch than those found anywhere else on the human body. This is probably because, due to the amount of time we spend on them, feet need to be well lubricated. It therefore stands to reason that we will lose a greater amount of sweat through the feet.

Since foot odour is caused by bacteria-digesting sweat, there are two main ways to reduce the risk of smelly feet. Firstly, reduce the amount of bacteria on your feet, which is quite simply a question of cleanliness. You can

and some more hints for sweaty feet...

- Wear well-ventilated shoes instead of closed shoes or boots.
- Wear pure cotton socks and socks made from absorbent material.
- Change your socks during the day.
- Apply an anti-perspirant to your feet.

help to control bacteria by washing your feet with a strong anti-bacterial soap and wearing clean socks. Secondly, curtail the amount of sweat that collects on your feet and in your shoes. Don't wear the same shoes every day; give them at least 24 hours to air. Try wearing all-leather shoes. Leather shoes 'breathe' whereas some artificial substances and rubber do not.

Footwear labels

Lining and sock – the inside of the shoe.

Leather or coated leather: An animal hide or skin, which may be treated with a coating.

Upper: The part of the shoe that you can see.

Textile: Fabric materials are natural or man-made.

Outer sole: The bottom part of the shoe, which will protect your foot from the ground.

Other material: Man-made materials such as rubber or PVC, usually used for the sole.

A CLOSE SHAVE

Why shave?

Ultimately it is a personal choice whether to shave or not, and how much or how often. Men shave on average about 20,000 times in a lifetime. It is thought by anthropologists that shaving the face improves the chances of finding a mate. Apparently men who shave on a regular basis are more likely to have sex than men who don't, which is one excellent reason to get the razor out. There are other reasons to shave of course; some find shaving a cleansing, rejuvenating, fresh experience. Personally I think a good wet shave takes years off my face! Whatever your reason for shaving, there are some tried-and-tested rules.

The fundamental principles of traditional wet shaving

A perfect shave should be achieved without cuts or irritation, while at the same time removing the beard.

1. **Bath or shower before shaving.** As with all types of shaving, it helps to soften the beard. This effect can also be achieved by soaking a folded face flannel in hot water and wrapping it around the face for a minute or so. This will soften the beard hairs and relax the skin so as to reduce the resistance while shaving. It is definitely recommended to shave after a hot shower, when the beard will be thoroughly soft and you can be sure that any dirt and possible germs

will be washed away and will not get worked into the skin during the shave.

2. **Leave the face wet**; this will leave a layer of water between the face and the soap. Apply your favourite shaving soap fairly generously. There are many types of soaps to choose from, to suit all skin types. Dip the tip of the brush in warm water and whip it around on the soap to create a good lather.

3. **Use a product that contains glycerine**, which will help lubricate and protect the skin. Avoid products that include alcohol, camphor, mint and menthol, potassium or sodium hydroxide, which are designed to force the hair up and away from the surface of the skin by swelling the hair follicle. Because the skin is slightly swollen, hair can become trapped under the skin when it recedes, which can lead to in-growing hairs. Alternatively, some quality gels are commendable; they are fast, moisturising and don't clog like some foams. Gels also help the razor to glide and, furthermore, come straight out of a pressurised can ready for use, making a brush unnecessary. But beware – if any product irritates, burns or tingles on your skin, don't use it.

4. **Flip the brush over the skin in an up and down motion** to evenly distribute the lather; this action will also help to lift the hairs. As for the shaving brush, almost any type will do – many high-quality brushes are made from silvertip badger hair, although this may not reconcile with everyone's views on using fur or animal hair.

5. **Warm the razor in hot water** before you start shaving. There are handfuls of different types of razors on the market. You should choose one that is suitable for your skin type, with a good weight and balance. The choices are disposables, cartridge razors (where blades are replaceable), the double-edged safety razor (that provides a close shave, but handle with care), and the classic 'cut-throat' razor (the name of which should be warning enough!) Don't discount disposable razors – obvious environmental issues aside, you can change them easily and cheaply and they are reasonably sharp. If you have an ongoing skin problem, you will minimise the chance of spreading an infection by changing your razor after every second shave.

6. **Shave with or across the grain**. That is to say, the direction in which the hairs grow. Some men can tolerate shaving against the grain but usually only after they have shaved once with the grain. Shaving against the grain can graze the skin and ultimately lead to 'razor burn' and in-growing hairs. Glide the razor over the skin, holding the skin taut with the free hand. Start at the sideburns and shave down one side, then repeat the exercise on the other side, then shave around the rest of the face. The hair over the top lip should be removed last; it is thicker than the other parts of the beard and the longer time the shaving soap has to soften the hairs the better. Rinse the razor regularly to avoid clogging. Use the hottest water that you can tolerate – it causes the metal blades to expand so that the sharp edge gets a little sharper and, of course, hot water will chase any

germs away. Check after this shave, rinse the face and, if needs be, shave again.

7. **Now rinse the face** with warm water, which will remove and dissolve any leftover shaving soap, then rinse in cold water to close the pores. Pat the skin dry with a clean towel, but do not rub as this can irritate freshly shaved skin.

8. **Moisturise.** A good wet shave exfoliates and cleanses the skin, leaving a fresh, healthy appearance. However, your skin needs to be protected from the elements so finally moisturise with a good-quality aftershave balm if you want to, or a facial moisturiser.

Dealing with cuts

Shaving in a hurry or using an old or damaged blade is the most common cause of shaving cuts. Even if you are very careful, cuts occur from time to time when bumps on the skin that are invisible to the eye get cut as the razor passes over them.

Rather than tear off tiny pieces of lavatory paper and stick them on the cut, use a styptic pencil to stem the flow of blood and help disinfect the skin.

Aftershave and eau de toilette

An aftershave can be a lotion, gel, balm or liquid. An alcohol-based astringent can also be used as an aftershave. It is normally used immediately after a shave and can contain an antiseptic such as alcohol to prevent the causes of infection, closing the pores and possibly numbing skin that has suffered minor cuts during the shave. Some have a moisturiser to soften the skin. Aftershaves can also contain a perfume, but not a huge amount, being typically one part essential oil to 40 or 50 parts alcohol.

Eau de toilette contains a larger amount of perfume concentrates, varying between 1 and 15 per cent. This combination gives a lighter but lasting scent, although one that does not linger as long as the more intense versions. Of all the men's fragrances, eau de toilette is the one that will last the longest but it is not meant to be used on the face – it was originally blended for use as a refreshing morning body splash. The terms eau de toilette and eau de Cologne are often used interchangeably, especially by Americans who seem to refer to all men's fragrances with the generic term 'cologne'.

Eau de Cologne, translated as 'water of Cologne', was originally formulated in Köln, Germany, by an Italian perfumer in 1709 and originally called *Kölnisch Wasser*. It gained popularity after Napoleon took to using it; apparently he used up to 54 bottles of his favourite cologne every month. Eau de Cologne is a blend of citrus and herbal oils in an ethanol base. Confusingly, some perfumers produce the same product but call it eau fraîche.

An eau de toilette should be worn very discreetly. Never pour on so much that it comes into a room before you.

The only time another person should be fully aware of the quality of your aftershave or eau de toilette is when they have their nose pressed up against your neck.

Check and test lots or fragrances before choosing one, because scents never smell quite the same on two different people. The choice of men's fragrances available as an eau de toilette is enormous, but your skin type will determine which product suits you best.

Designer stubble

To get designer stubble you should shave every couple of days to keep the shadow look without it developing into a full beard. Alternatively, a set of clippers similar to those used by hairdressers are quite cheap and easily available. Using clippers means you can keep the hair at acceptable levels without having to shave back to the skin. Try to choose clippers that are adjustable so you can select the length of hair required.

If you use clippers, trim the hairs in the direction of the beard growth. Avoid applying too much pressure or you could risk making your stubble look patchy. Pay attention to the speed at which your hair grows; if it grows quickly, you'll need to trim it more often. Unfortunately, the upkeep of designer stubble is an ongoing process – you can't just shape it and leave it.

While you are growing the beard out, you should fight the urge to cut it straight back. It will itch a lot when it gets to a certain level of growth, due to the unfamiliar feeling of having hair this close to your skin. It is extremely important to keep the skin clean, cleanse the skin daily and keep your beard clean with a hair shampoo. The itching will pass. When it does, it is still important to keep the skin and hair clean.

If you want to maintain a neater look, establish a line on the neck and shave below this line regularly.

and some more hints on maintaining the designer stubble look...

- Ditch the scruffy clothes. Three days' worth of beard growth combined with scruffy clothing will be simply too much; you will look unkempt and dishevelled. You are going for the rugged look, not the un-groomed and smelly look. The same applies to intentionally messy haircuts.
- Keep your beard clean and well groomed. You can use the same shampoo as you do for your hair and, after you've washed it, make sure you rinse the shampoo out thoroughly.
- Watch for razor bumps, where the hair grows a little bit then turns back on itself, pushing into a pore in your skin and creating an angry-looking bump. The best treatment is to remove the offending hair using tweezers. Comb your beard regularly to stop razor bumps occurring.

In-growing hairs

The correct medical term for in-growing hairs is *pseudofoliculitis barbae* and people with curly hair seem to be the most susceptible. When you shave, the hair follicle is left in the skin. As it continues to grow out, it turns back and grows into the surrounding skin. The in-grown hair causes a slight bump and, the next time you shave, the bump is cut off, causing bleeding and possibly an infection. There are few products that can effectively deal with the problem but you could try soaking a face flannel in hot water and holding against the skin for a few moments then, very carefully, using sterilised tweezers, pluck out the in-grown hair. Resist the temptation to pull the whole hair out, but just pluck out the loose end. If you pull the whole thing out the skin can heal over and when the hair grows back you will have the same situation – a hair caught under the skin.

and some hints on avoiding in-growing hairs...

- Don't pull on the skin during the shave. This encourages the beard hair to come out further. Once cut, the hair sits lower in the skin, increasing the in-growing risk.
- Shave in the direction of the hair growth, as the shave won't be as close.
- If the problem is especially bad, miss a shave occasionally or try using an electric razor.

Very schick — electric razors

For that zinging, just shaved feeling, nothing really gets
as close as a wet shave. However, shaving with an electric
razor is definitely a viable alternative. Manufacturers of
electric shavers will tell you that, because the razor rolls
up the skin in front of the blades and forces the hair
further out just before it is cut, you will in fact get
a smoother shave from an electric razor.

We have Colonel Jacob Schick, an American, to thank for
the electric or 'dry razor'. His model, launched in 1931,
was the first ever successful one-handed dry razor.

For optimum success with the electric razor, follow
these points:

1. As with all types of shaving, the best advice is to bath
    or shower beforehand. In common with wet shaving,
    electric shaving is also improved if the beard is softer.
    If washing is not possible, splash on an alcohol-based
    pre-shave lotion, which helps the hairs to stand out
    further and to remove oils from the skin.
2. Gently rub over your beard with your fingers to find
    out in which direction the beard grows – it nearly
    always varies from one part of the face to another.
3. Now pull the skin gently with one hand, while
    dragging the shaver against the direction of growth
    with the other; this will give the closest shave.
4. Finally, use an aftershave moisturiser to keep the
    skin moist.

Shaving with an electric razor or battery model is particularly good for people who cannot risk cutting themselves and for those who don't heal so quickly or are taking blood-thinning medications. It is also useful for anyone with unsteady hands, who run the risk of serious cuts if shaving with a blade.

Electric shaving is an absolute must for the perpetually late and for gentlemen who have been up all night hanging around a roulette table and haven't been home. And for cab drivers apparently. I saw one in London some years ago narrowly miss a pedestrian as he lifted his head to reach under his chin with a battery-operated contraption.

Body shaving or waxing

Fashionable at the moment and gaining ground but remains absolutely down to personal preference, patience and, I would imagine, razor-handling ability. There is the view that a hairless body is more hygienic, but this look is not for everyone – in some areas the after-effects can be indescribably itchy, so I'm told.

WORD OF MOUTH

Hollywood smiles are legendary: think George Clooney or Julia Roberts. They all have well-kept, fabulous grins. The red carpet at any film premiere night is like a dental convention, with huge, pearly grins flashing beautiful white teeth in every direction. It is very simple – clean, bright teeth project wealth, health, happiness and success and, what's more, youth and vitality. In the movies, only serial killers and peasants have yellow teeth and gaps.

Dental hygiene is such an important part of our daily body-care routine. Failure to brush and floss and look after the oral cavity leads inevitably to tooth decay and infection and ultimately, of course, eventual tooth loss and extremely bad breath. After spending almost five years training at the Royal Dental Hospital in the 1970s and seeing at first hand the aftermath of basic dental neglect, I for one brush and floss at every opportunity throughout the day to maintain my red carpet grin!

The alternatives once your teeth are lost are not necessarily very comfortable, certainly not always very good looking and, in the case of implants, not cheap. Dental technicians are extremely artistic people and some materials available today are truly amazing, but plastic teeth will always look like plastic teeth. So that is another reason to look after your originals, if not the best reason. Go to an interview or to a meeting or kiss a friend on the cheek when you have foul breath and everyone who notices the smell will recoil. What on earth is the point of washing, putting on clean clothes

and then having terrible-smelling breath, just
because you are too lazy to clean your mouth?

Oral hygiene

Your face is the first thing that other people look
at when they meet you and all of it should be clean,
inside and out. Achieving a fresh, healthy mouth
through cleaning is not difficult. There are dozens
of products on the market to help us, the most basic
being the toothbrush and learning how to use one
correctly is a must. In the years I spent working in
dentistry in Germany during the late 1970s there
were allegedly more cars per household in Bavaria
than toothbrushes; hard to prove perhaps but it may
have accounted for the amount of work I had to do!

and some more hints on good oral hygiene...

- Go to your dentist every six months for a check up.
- Brush at least twice a day and floss and rinse.
- Always brush before going to bed.
- Use a fluoride rinse or one containing hydrogen
  peroxide to clean and rinse off stains after eating.
- Quit smoking! Smoking is extremely bad for the
  teeth, the bones and the gums, and leaves stains
  that are virtually impossible to remove.

There are dozens of toothpastes promising all kinds of benefits, including snow-white teeth. Some of these claims may be true, who knows, but the best policy is simply using a toothpaste, brushing at least twice a day, and brushing properly. A good routine is a mouth rinse, then tooth brushing, then flossing, followed by a mouth rinse, preferably using a mouthwash that is low in alcohol. Minimise the intake of foods and drinks that can stain your teeth easily, for example, coffee, tea, red wine and some dark carbonated drinks. Drinks that stain are often acidic and can soften the outer layer of the tooth enamel, allowing the stain to set, while saliva and fluoride help to harden tooth enamel.

Guide to brushing

Brushing twice a day for two minutes is probably the key to oral hygiene. It is recommended that you change your toothbrush every three months. When selecting a new toothbrush, choose one with a comfortable handle and a brush head small enough to reach the areas that are difficult to get to. Always brush from gum to tooth with a rotating wrist action. Do not brush up and down gum to tooth, tooth to gum or scrub along the labial (the side facing your lips), buccal (the side facing your cheeks) or palatal (the side facing your palate), as this will only encourage gum recession and wear away at parts of the teeth not protected by enamel.

Start with the outer surfaces of your lower teeth, work from the back teeth to the front and then right round to the back teeth on the other side. Once you have finished all the outer surfaces, repeat the process for the inner surfaces and when you have finished that, do the whole thing again for the upper teeth. Finally brush the biting surfaces. Be gentle, remembering that a worn brush and excessive pressure will damage tooth enamel.

Brushing

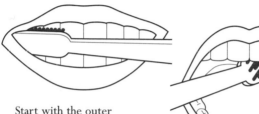

Start with the outer surfaces of the teeth.

Work from the back teeth to the front, then around to the other side.

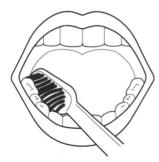

Next, brush the inner surfaces in the same way.

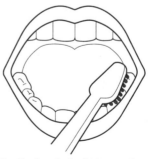

Finally, brush the biting surfaces.

Guide to flossing

Floss gently and as low as possible down between each tooth, but be careful not to cut your gums. Move the floss around your teeth and with a little pressure slide the floss up and down the tooth surface.

Flossing

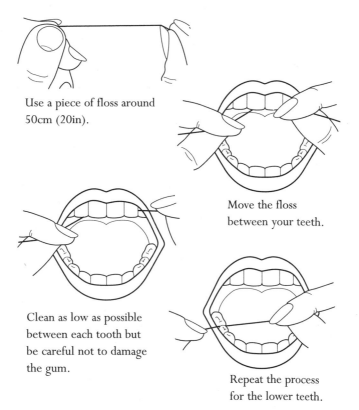

Use a piece of floss around 50cm (20in).

Move the floss between your teeth.

Clean as low as possible between each tooth but be careful not to damage the gum.

Repeat the process for the lower teeth.

Mouthwash

A daily anti-bacterial mouthwash, containing, for example, chlorhexidine or cetylpyridinium chloride, can help protect against the growth of bacteria in the mouth. If bacteria are allowed to develop, a build-up of plaque can occur, which is a major cause of gum disease and cavities. A daily mouthwash can care for the gums, help fight bad breath by reducing the bacteria that cause it and, if it contains fluoride, can also strengthen the teeth and provide daily cavity protection. Always ask your dentist about a suitable mouthwash because some can actually stain the teeth.

Tongue cleaning

It is estimated that 70 per cent of the bacteria in the human oral cavity thrives on the tongue and is in part responsible for periodontal disease, plaque on the teeth, tooth decay, gum recession and gum infections, eventual tooth loss and bad breath.

A tongue cleaner, tongue brush or tongue scraper is an oral hygiene tool designed to remove bacterial build-up from food debris, fungi and dead cells from the surface of the tongue. Ayurveda, which is the oldest system of medicine in the world today, has for centuries recommended that tongue cleaning should be part of the daily washing regimen. Ergonomically shaped tongue scrapers are designed to conform to the anatomic shape of the tongue to clean the surface of the tongue.

As quoted in the Journal of Clinical Microbiology in February 2003, there are some 500 different types of bacteria on the human tongue and therefore tongue cleaning is generally viewed as the solution for halitosis and bad breath. Scientific study has shown that, in 80–95 per cent of cases, bad breath is caused by bacteria at the rear of the tongue. Further research has shown that, of the rest, 5–20 per cent of cases originate in the stomach or from the tonsils and from decaying food stuck between the teeth. Clinical trials have shown that using a tongue scraper daily has a significant effect on eliminating anaerobic bacteria and decreasing oral malodour.

Electric toothbrushes

The tried-and-tested hand-held toothbrush is probably still the best type of brush. You control it and it doesn't need batteries. Electric toothbrushes promise all sorts of things; they are said to remove more plaque, get into the difficult-to-access areas and so on, which is all fine and good, but the standard hand-held, battery-free model, used properly, will do exactly the same and it is a lot easier to carry around. But of course it is all down to personal choice or possibly the depth of your pockets.

Care of dentures

It is important to keep full or partial dentures clean at all times. You should remove them at night to give the gums a rest. It is highly recommended that you brush dentures to remove debris and to avoid build-up and stains. Brush them gently over a basin of cold water (in case you drop them) with a toothbrush specifically designed for cleaning dentures and a small amount of toothpaste. Keep them in a glass of cold water when you are not wearing them. Always brush them before you put them back into your mouth. Ask your dentist to clean them for you if the stains have become too difficult to remove.

Crowns and bridges

To care for crowns and bridgework you need to brush and floss twice daily. The following instructions should help you with flossing:

1. Use a bridge floss threader; a flexible piece of plastic with a loop to thread the floss.
2. Thread a 35cm (14in) piece of floss through the loop; leave one side half as long as the other.
3. Insert the end of the flosser without the hole in between the bridge and the gum.
4. Hold the longer piece of floss and gently bring it up, and bring the pointed end all the way through.
5. Use both hands to floss and move the floss back and forth under the bridge, from one end to the other, and finally have a rinse.

SKIN-CARE
ESSENTIALS

Fortunately the days have long gone when husbands and boyfriends had to secretly nick a dollop of face cream from their wives and girlfriends. The shops these days are full of specialised products aimed only at men. Also long gone, at least for those men who are already up to speed, are the hang-ups about using moisturisers. No, it's not just for girls – far from it, it's necessary! Some of us realised the benefits years ago. So, unless you want skin that looks like a crocodile suitcase in later life, or you want a face with so many creases and lines it resembles a route map, some attention to your skin is required.

To be fair, most men do have the right idea when it comes to grooming and personal hygiene with plenty of attention given to the gym, the suit, the aftershave and which trendy hair gel to plop on, but skincare is often completely forgotten.

A lot of men would probably raise an eyebrow at the mention of skincare or mutter something like 'That's for the girlies; all I need is a shave'. Well it's time to think again. Skin is the largest organ in the body. In the average person it weighs about 3kg (7lb) and covers an area, on average, of approximately $2m^2$ ($21ft^2$). Male skin is about 15 per cent oilier than female skin and has larger pores. It's not just a covering to hold everything together, the main function of the skin is to protect us from a very harsh environment. So it needs some attention.

The first step is to establish what sort of skin you have and then customise your choice of washing and moisturising products to suit your skin type. If you don't have any significant skin problems apart from the occasional spot then the chances are you have normal skin.

A recurrence of blackheads, acne or even whiteheads is a sign that you have oily skin. The skin may even shine a little but, with ongoing use of the correct products, it can be returned to a normal skin. Dry skin can feel uncomfortable and tight after washing and will benefit from a moisturiser. Dry skin tends to age faster and skin wrinkles are more noticeable. Combination skin is obviously a mixture of both skin types and needs more attention; finding the right product for this type of skin can be a case of trial and error.

Moisturisers soothe the skin, especially after shaving, and protect the skin from the elements. A good moisturiser has numerous benefits but mostly it works by duplicating and strengthening the role of your body's own naturally produced sebum. Sebum is your skin's restorative fluid and thus protects your skin from excessive moisture loss. A quick moisturise the 'morning after the night before' is therefore an absolute must, as the dehydrating effect of excessive booze and tobacco on the skin are catastrophic. Moisturisers also help to reduce the appearance of wrinkles and lines. Using a moisturising product that offers protection from the harmful rays of the sun is also important.

Fighting the signs of ageing

Keeping skin free from irritants helps the healing process. Washing can be anti-ageing because it increases the circulation, which in turn aids cell regeneration, thus slowing the signs of ageing. Combating the things that damage the skin the most, such as sunshine, wind and free radicals is a big step in the right direction.

Smoking tobacco and the effects of the sun are two of the biggest hazards that should be avoided and not just for the benefit of your skin. If you need any proof of what can happen after too much sun exposure, just look around the airport at the end of the summer as swathes of tourists with leathery skins return from their holidays!

and more hints on fighting the signs of ageing...

- Moisturise every day after a shave; this really is the best and most basic advice.
- Don't use the same moisturiser for the skin under your eyes as you use on the rest of the face, as it can drag the more delicate skin there and age it faster.
- Pure vitamin E cream or aloe vera oil will give an intensive moisturising treatment.
- Drink plenty of water to moisturise from the inside.
- Always use a sun cream if you are out in the fresh air – in winter as well as summer – or a moisturiser that has a good level of ultra-violet protection.

The eyes have it

The skin around the eyes is the thinnest on the body so treat it very gently and keep friction to a minimum. Because the eyes are constantly moving, wear and tear is increased and apt to show the signs of ageing faster than anywhere else. Always use a lighter moisturiser around the eyes than you would for the rest of the face.

Eye cream or gel will help to reduce wrinkles and dark circles under the eyes caused by fatigue. Use the tip of one finger to dab on the cream as this skin is sensitive. Don't rub your eyes it will put the skin under more pressure. Never exfoliate (see page 68) around the eyes and don't smoke, as the effects show very quickly in the skin around the eye.

Puffiness around the eyes can be caused by fatigue or late nights and too little sleep; a cool eye gel can help as does drinking plenty of water. That irritating twitch we get sometimes under or at the corner of an eye is caused by a temporary chemical imbalance in the body and occurs most frequently when we are tired, under stress or have over-indulged in caffeine or nicotine. The problem, correctly called myokymia, can appear anywhere in the body, but is particularly annoying in the eye. Proper nutrition and rest usually see it off.

Lips

The skin covering the lips is very thin, allowing the colour in the blood vessels to show through, hence the characteristic colour. They do not have sweat glands and rely on saliva for moisture. If the saliva evaporates too quickly, chapped lips are the result; lip balms go some way to stopping this effect. Use a lip balm when out and about, preferably one that contains a sun protection factor upwards of SPF15. Lips do not contain melanin and therefore do not tan, making them susceptible to the rigours of sunshine. Take particular care to use a lip balm with sun protection before you strap on the snowboard or weigh anchor.

Facial scrubs

Exfoliation is the process of removing dead cells from the outermost layer of the skin and it is a useful process to help keep your skin healthy and clean. Use a facial scrub to remove excess dead cells, and help reduce the appearance and development of acne blemishes. Avoid scrubs that contain ingredients such as crushed nut kernels or seeds, which are thought to be too rough.

Massage the scrub mix gently into your face and neck and rinse off with warm water.

Shaving is one of the best exfoliating exercises and may explain why men tend to have fewer wrinkles in that part of the face than women.

Clay masks

Some men might feel a bit self-conscious applying a clay mask, but the effects are very good. Clay masks will improve texture and tone and remove oil and dirt from the pores.

Clean the face, then rinse in warm water to open the pores. Apply a thin layer of clay mask to the whole face and let it dry. Rinse the dried clay off with warm water and pat the face dry with a clean towel.

and some more hints for keeping your skin looking healthy and younger...

- Drink plenty of water.
- Eat healthily.
- Do not smoke.
- Always use sunscreen or sunblock.

Sun care

You must have been living on another planet not to have heard by now that unprotected overexposure to the sun is extremely dangerous and in extreme cases can lead to cancer of the skin.

Sunburn results when the amount of exposure to sunshine exceeds the body's ability to protect the skin. The body's protective pigment, melanin, is not always strong enough to protect against the sun's harmful rays. In some very light-skinned people sunburn can occur after as little as 15 minutes of exposure. Wearing creams containing high levels of protective ingredients – an SPF or sun protection factor – coupled with protective clothing, a wide-brimmed hat and sunglasses are good ways to protect the skin and eyes.

Sunscreen
The positive side of being out in the sunshine can't be ignored. We derive vitamin D from exposure to the sun and, generally, after being in the sun we tend to feel happier, more confident, more attractive and healthier. The sun emits two types of ultra-violet rays that you should be aware of: UVA, which is ageing and UVB, which can burn. Both are potentially highly dangerous to the skin. The best sunscreens will protect the skin from a wide spectrum of UV rays and typically contain substances such as avonbenzone, titanium dioxide or zinc oxide. Some products only protect against UVA and with these you will tan but you might burn.

Aftersun creams

Mainly formulated to extend the life of the tan, aftersun creams also go some way to cooling the damaging effects of overexposure. But use them lightly as it is possible to put on too much. A good aftersun cream will have a lightweight texture and will hydrate the skin without suffocating it.

Sunbeds or sunlamps

People who suffer the excruciating horrors of skin complaints such as psoriasis and eczema are sometimes given courses of treatment with lamps or on beds that emit artificial versions of the sun's useful rays. In some cases it is noticeably beneficial. I feel that there have been too many adverse reports in the media to justify lying around on sunbeds for any other reason than on medical grounds.

Bronzing creams

If you want a year-round tan, bronzing creams might provide a cheaper option than regular flights to beach-side destinations. Bronzing or self-tanning creams will make your skin look tanned, but do not give you any of the healthy things we derive from natural sunshine. Use such products carefully as they can make you look a ridiculous colour with over-use and are, after all, laden with chemicals.

DIET AND
WELL-BEING

*All human history attests
That happiness for man,
The hungry sinner;
Since Eve ate apples,
Much depends on dinner*

Lord Byron in *Don Juan*

Kick Start the Day

Kick-start the day with a good breakfast! After a night's sleep the brain, as well as the body, is running on empty. In most people the brain represents about 3 per cent of the body weight but consumes as much as 17 per cent of the body's total energy and thus needs refuelling quickly after waking up.

A study carried out at the University of Bristol examined the breakfast habits of 126 volunteers between the ages of 20 and 79 and assessed their mental health. It was found that those who ate breakfast every day were less depressed, less emotionally distressed and had much lower perceived levels of stress compared with those who missed the first meal of the day.

A good breakfast will benefit mood, mental and physical performance, maintenance of a healthy weight and general wellbeing. If breakfast is missed, it is unlikely that subsequent meals during the day will compensate for the nutrients that have been lost, so the old proverb, 'Breakfast like a king, lunch like a prince and dine like a pauper', still holds true.

Five a Day

We all know by now that at least 'five a day' is the recommended number of fruit and vegetables everyone should eat for a healthy lifestyle. There is a huge variety of fruit and vegetables to choose from, all year long. They are relatively inexpensive to buy fresh and are not beyond the reach of everyone.

There are five good reasons to eat five portions of fruit and vegetables every day:

1. They're packed with vitamins and minerals.
2. They can help you to maintain a healthy weight.
3. They're an excellent source of fibre and antioxidants.
4. They help reduce the risk of heart disease, stroke and some cancers.
5. They taste good.

Almost all fruit and vegetables count towards your five a day. What's more, there's no limit to how much you can consume – so the more you eat, the better. It's also good to know that you should eat a variety of fruit and vegetables to get the maximum nutritional benefits. This is because they each contain different combinations of fibre, vitamins, minerals and other nutrients. Besides, eating the same ones every day could be boring. You probably won't have to dramatically change your diet to reach the recommended amount of fruit and vegetables you should eat. Fruit and vegetables can be found in many things you eat, even in takeaways and ready meals. You just need to know where to look.

Ready meals, convenience foods and takeaways are often high in added salt, sugar or fat and should only be eaten in moderation — so it's important to check the nutritional information on food labels.

and some more hints for making sure you get your 'five a day'...

- Fresh, frozen, chilled, canned, 100 per cent juice and smoothies all count, as do dried fruit and vegetables.
- Fruit and vegetables don't have to be eaten on their own to count. You can also include vegetables in soups, stews, casseroles and other dishes.
- Fruit and vegetables contained in convenience foods, such as ready meals, pasta sauces, soups and puddings, also contribute to your five a day. However, these ready-made foods can be high in salt, sugar and fat, which should only ever be eaten in moderation, so it's important to check the nutrition information given.
- Dietary supplements such as vitamins and minerals do not count towards five a day. This is because many dietary supplements don't have the same nutritional benefits as fruit and vegetables.
- Potatoes and other related vegetables such as yams and cassava do not count. This is because they are classified as starchy foods.

Water

The British Dietetic Association has recommend that the average adult should drink 1.5–2.5 litres (roughly 6–8 glasses) of water a day and increase this amount following vigorous exercise or during periods of hot weather. You can get some of your daily requirements from sources other than pure water, from a cup of tea for example. Water is the main ingredient of all drinks including carbonated and still drinks and fruit juices.

Amazingly, it is possible to drink too much water; initial signs of over-hydration include nausea, dizziness, apathy and confusion. Strangely, these are some of the same problems that come about from dehydration so it is a good idea to be aware of how much you are drinking.

and some more hints for maintaining your wellbeing...

- Never go food shopping when you are hungry as it is tempting to buy more food than you need.
- Limit stimulants like caffeine, alcohol and refined sugar in your diet.
- Limit the amount of times you dine out.
- The best advice to avoid the onset of obesity is to eat less.

HOW TO DRESS: THE ART OF LOOKING GOOD

*Clothes don't make a man but clothes
have got many a man a good job.*

Herbert Harold Vreeland

Savile Row in London will always be the spiritual home of the fine British suit. The estate occupies a corner near Bond Street. Created in 1695 by Lord Burlington, and the street named after his wife Lady Dorothy Savile, it has been patronised for centuries by royalty and the famous – Winston Churchill, Lord Nelson and Napoleon III all shopped there. The expression 'bespoke' originated in Savile Row; it is the name given to a piece of cloth that has been sold and therefore is spoken for.

How to look good in a suit

Suits are worn for a variety of reasons; special occasions, job interviews, funerals and, of course, as our everyday workwear. You can improve your image by wearing your clothes properly. The first step is to remove the maker's label from the sleeve of your new suit if it has one; leaving it sewn on for all to see is not classy, no matter how phenomenally 'designer' the suit may be. You will never need a label to prove anything if the suit fits you properly and you don't slouch around in it.

An ill-fitting suit can be a disaster, so make sure your suit fits. Ask your outfitter for advice, they will know best.

Subtlety
Don't wear an odd-coloured suit. Wear a simple neutral colour such as grey, black or navy or add a different dimension with a pinstripe. If the suit is fairly neutral

it will give you an opportunity to wear ties of a stronger colour. Choose a shirt that is of a similar tone, such as powder blue or even pink, as this always works the best.

Don't be tempted to make a suit out of two fairly well-matched pieces. Although technically the same colour, the two pieces will never quite match and people will notice that it is not really a suit. A simple solution is, if you need a suit, buy a suit!

Basic suit shapes

Single-breasted with two buttons.

Single-breasted with three buttons.

Double-breasted with two buttons.

Double-breasted with three buttons.

and some more hints for looking good in a suit...

- Keep your clothes and your suit well-pressed at all times.
- If you are a shorter person, wear a single-breasted jacket; double-breasted styles give the appearance of the person drowning in the material and can make you look smaller.
- If you are larger around the middle, wear a lower-buttoning jacket as it will give you a longer silhouette.
- The collar of the jacket should fit so that 6mm (¼in) of shirt is visible when you are standing. This will ensure that your shirt is not engulfed when you sit down.
- Armholes in the jacket should be high enough so that when you raise your arms over your head the jacket does not ride up over your face.
- Trousers should fit well at the waist and without the need for a belt. Trousers should not be tight on the thighs. The fit should allow free movement and, when standing, allow the pressed crease to hang uninterrupted. The length of the leg (the inside leg measurement) should allow the bottom to break on the shoe and 'stack' slightly with about one crease or fold.
- Your waistcoat, if you wear one, should fit so that it sits just below the waistband of the trousers. It must fit well but should not be so tight as to pull at the buttons. The bottom button of a waistcoat is never fastened.

- Dark socks and perfectly polished shoes are a must. Don't wear socks that are lighter than the colour of the suit.
- Your shoe colour should match your belt colour.
- Always wear a matching belt with a suit. Black is usually the best choice except for lighter summer suits in khaki, beige and so on, when a brown belt is probably more suitable.
- Your belt buckle should be discrete. A buckle suitable for the jeans of a Texan cowhand, for example, may be considered misplaced.
- Any accessories that you may be wearing, such as a watch, should be in a matching metal and should not clash with the metal of the belt buckle.
- You should never wear a belt with a waistcoat.
- If you are wearing a waistcoat and a jacket you do not have to fasten the jacket.
- If you are wearing a jacket, fastened and without a waistcoat, always unfasten it when you sit down. Pull your trousers up very slightly at the knee at the same time to avoid a ballooning of the fabric at the knee when you stand up. Re-fasten your jacket when you stand up.
- Two-button jackets should be fastened with the top button only. Three-button jackets are fastened with the middle button only and the top button if so desired.
- You should never fasten the bottom button on any jacket.

Shirts

First and foremost, wear a well-ironed, clean dress shirt every day and, if needs be, change into a new one during the day. Cut, colour and collar shape is certainly a matter of personal choice.

You should be able to fit one finger between your shirt collar and your neck and no more. Button all the buttons on a dress shirt and button all of the buttons at the cuffs. Your shirt is too small if it pulls at the chest buttons.

The shirt cuffs should not ride up when you stretch your arms. A button cuff should break exactly at the wrist whereas a double cuff or, as the Americans would say, a French cuff, should break about 12mm (½in) further down and should be fastened with cufflinks.

Always fasten your cuffs. If you are wearing double cuffs, wear the best cufflinks you can afford to hold the cuffs together, but obviously they should not be too enormous. Double cuffs will look slightly ridiculous undone and hanging out of the end of your suit jacket sleeve, not to mention a nuisance. Only show enough cuff to keep the cufflinks visible and that is all. However, these are not always hard-and-fast rules because constantly changing fashion trends and suit designs tend to set the current standard.

Tuck your shirt in and keep it tucked in. A shirt hanging out looks childish and, particularly in the case of hotel waiters, unbelievably sloppy! A gentleman wouldn't dream of wearing a dress shirt outside any style of trousers.

Some people assert that a monogrammed shirt is a must for the successful businessman. Why a monogram is important for the successful man is hard to say, unless of course the wearer happens to suffer from amnesia. If you want to wear monogrammed things, the monogram should be discreet and never on a cuff, being best positioned on a shirt pocket where at least the jacket will cover it up.

(*Note*: Follow the guidelines on page 102 for the perfectly ironed shirt).

Ties

Most people still wear, and are expected to wear, a necktie if the work situation or formal situation demands it. In some circles, however, they are going very slowly out of fashion. All men have the potential to look good in a tie; unfortunately the wrong tie can also make the wrong impression. A tie can make a statement about a person even before the first handshake.

There are several knot choices and the one you choose depends on your shirt collar and personal preference. The Windsor knot is probably the broadest knot and looks best with a spread-collar shirt. The half-Windsor looks good on both a conventional collar and the spread-collar shirt. The easiest to tie by far and the most familiar is the four-in-hand and, although it is said to be school-boyish and therefore possibly less manly than the Windsor pair, the four-in-hand is worn by at least 80 per cent of tie wearers (for instructions on how to tie a four-in-hand, see page 88).

Don't wear a tie that is too short, as it looks strange, as does one that is so long you have to tuck its tail into your trousers. Just shy of your belt is fine. Tie the tie so that the tail is just hidden by the front of the tie, not the other way round. Most ties are made with a loop at the back of the front part; use this to tuck the tail in if you want to.

Be careful with your tie choice: a bold colour statement is less conventional and says a lot about your character. This is no bad thing, but just be careful it doesn't become the centre of attention and detract from the overall impression of the suit. Check occasionally that your tie knot is still tied properly and hasn't slipped undone – nothing shouts 'sloppy' more than a fallen knot. Check after eating that there is no food on it.

Unless you really have to, avoid the novelty variety and remember that clip-ons are not an option in the adult world.

(*Note*: See page 110–111 for information about how to care for ties).

How to tie a four-in-hand knot

1. Place the tie around your neck with the widest part on the right and hanging down further than the narrow end.
2. Holding the narrow end, take the wide end and pass it over the narrow end to the left and then under the narrow end to the right.
3. Pass the wide end back over to the left again.
4. Pass the wide end underneath the half-formed knot. With your left hand pass the wide end from underneath over the half knot and pull the wider end through to the front.
5. Pass the wide end of the tie between the outer layer of the knot and the layer directly underneath it and pull through. Hold the narrow end of the tie firmly and tighten the knot.

When the knot is finished the ends should be a similar length or with the narrow end slightly shorter, and finish just above the belt line. The standard length of a tie is approximately 1.4m (57in) and, although the four-in-hand uses less tie material to form the knot, a standard tie could still be too short for the taller person; it would be wrong to have the narrow end finish mid-chest. Outfitters for taller people generally stock longer ties.

Four-in-hand knot

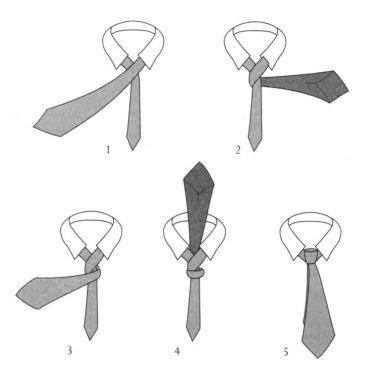

1

2

3

4

5

Tie pins

Tie tacks, tie chains, tie pins and slides could make you look as if you are trying too hard and some can look very tacky indeed. Try to avoid wearing a tie pin at all, especially the novelty variety.

Blue jeans

Jeans were made popular by American kids in the 1950s.
The material was first made in France and called *serge de
Nîmes*; later the serge was made into trousers for sailors
working out of Genoa in Italy and was named *bleu de
Gênes*, which over time became simply 'jeans'. Modern
jeans incorporating rivets are said to have been designed
by Levi Strauss in San Francisco in the 1850s to make
gold miners' work trousers more robust. Japanese
selvedge denim, woven from a single thread, is now
considered to be the best in the world. The late Yves
Saint Laurent famously said:

> *I have often said that I wished I had invented blue
> jeans; the most spectacular, the most practical, the most
> relaxed, nonchalant. They have expression, modesty, sex
> appeal, simplicity — all I hope for in my clothes.*

After reading that, I thought, what else can you say?
Except, don't wear polished shoes with them and
never iron a crease in them.

Be sure of dress codes before you go out; some dining
rooms will still ban entry if you are wearing jeans or
do not have a tie. The fact that your designer jeans were
hand sewn in Milan will interest no one — rules are rules.

Underwear confidential

Clinical evidence is mixed when it comes to suggesting the best type of underwear for a man. It has long been thought that wearing tight underwear negatively affects the production of mature sperm cells. It is a fact that overheating the testicles can result in impaired sperm production and it is also true that the ideal temperature for sperm production is slightly lower than the core body temperature, which would probably account for their natural location. Tight underwear that holds everything close to the body may keep things a bit too warm, although, as the underwear is not worn all the time, this may not be too detrimental. It has been suggested that loose-fitting boxer-style underwear is the best from a health perspective.

The choice is yours, but the most important thing to remember is that, whatever you choose, your underwear should be immaculately clean and changed every day. Never tuck your shirt into it and never, ever wear a dark vest under a shirt so that it shows through.

Beachwear

Again, the choice is yours, but do beware of mini styles, such as tight racing trunks and shapes that accentuate the bulge or advertise the lack of one. These styles can look very crude if you are not careful and you would need to have a very good, toned figure to carry them off. Swimming shorts are a safer bet as they tend to be a lot more flattering to all figures. Don't forget that spandex is only for cyclists.

Warm weather

The practice of removing your shirt in public places other than on a beach should be avoided at all costs. This misplaced behaviour is another on the list of things not to do and is seen in towns and cities everywhere as soon as the sun comes out. It is an offence that is usually committed by those who really shouldn't. Even when you think it's safe to remove your shirt, in the most private of situations – in a back garden other than your own, for example – you may be offending the sensitive.

It is considered extremely ill mannered to sit in a street café or come to a table minus your shirt shirt, even at home. Never, ever take your shirt off and wander around town. Wearing a vest instead of a shirt in sunny weather is not acceptable either.

Wearing of a white handkerchief with a knot tied at each corner, reminiscent of a Monty Python sketch, is unthinkable even if you have forgotten your sun hat.

Jacket removal

It is considered very bad manners for the gentleman to remove his jacket during a formal event but, should hot or humid weather dictate, the ranking man – for example a member of the royal family or the guest of honour – may give permission to the rest by removing his jacket.

Rolling up your sleeves

Rolling up the shirt sleeves has always suggested getting down to work. I still work with my sleeves rolled up – it is very comfortable, does not look too casual and avoids the risk of having soaking wet cuffs at the end of the evening. I can see nothing wrong with it.

Two turns up on a dress shirt is fine, rolled so that the shirt material is on the outside, not on the inside. Unbutton the cuff and roll back in folds that are the width of the cuff and no more, the turned back cuff will stay put.

Dressing your age

The old expression 'mutton dressed as lamb' is usually reserved for women. It is a bit harsh, but it does go to show that not dressing your age can attract some pretty vicious comments. In our culture it's a good idea to stay away from the clothes that the younger generation are wearing; it is lamentable to see older men dressed in clothes obviously designed for teenagers.

DEPORTMENT

*What is a fine person of beauteous face, unless
deportment gives them decent grace.*

Winston Churchill

How you look is important, of course, but how you carry yourself (and how you carry off what you are wearing) is also paramount. This is the essence of deportment. Slouch into a room wearing an expensive designer suit and you might just as well have come in wearing one from a supermarket.

Look at some facts; 90 per cent of the signals we send are not verbal. It is said time and time again to people going to job interviews – or any meeting for that matter – that you have approximately three seconds in which to make a good impression and that you never get a second chance to make that first impression. Clichés they may be, but we all do it without thinking – it is human nature to pigeonhole a person the instant we look at them. You may be carrying a briefcase full of university certificates and have a CV that will impress the interviewer, but they are all utterly useless if you walk into a room like you've the weight of the world on your shoulders. The importance of standing and walking correctly cannot be stressed enough.

Posture

Deportment has been taught in finishing schools, such as the famous Lucie Clayton Academy (no relation to the author) in Kensington, London, since the late 1920s. Students were encouraged to walk around the class with books on their heads and a broom handle held horizontally across the back and through the arms to learn how to carry themselves well and develop good deportment. To make the point clear to trainee butlers, the late Ivor Spencer MBE asked students at his butler school in London to walk around the room with a champagne glass balanced on their heads to encourage the old standard of head up and shoulders back.

The way you carry yourself, when correct, will project body language that displays success, confidence, high self-esteem and above all pride; it will set you apart immediately from those who slouch around, round shouldered and with their hands in the pockets.

As already noted, 90 per cent of the signals we send out are not verbal. The way you walk and carry yourself is as clear a message to anyone watching as the way you hold a knife and fork; you simply cannot hide your body language and it will categorise you in seconds. Look in any tailor's shop window: all the suits and jackets are shown on upright and perfectly shaped mannequins.

Since antiquity, rules for deportment have guided the behaviour of the more privileged classes and the people who served them. With this in mind, here are a few of the simple points that are taught to butlers and are indeed useful for everyone:

- Walk with a straight back and don't stoop or have round shoulders. However, you don't have to walk around as if you are on a military parade ground.
- Walk and stand with your head up, but not with your head held high in a lofty or haughty manner, as you will appear aloof and arrogant.
- Walk and stand with your shoulders back.
- Walk meaningfully and in a slightly assertive way; this will make you seem purposeful rather than frightened.
- Your clothes will look better on you if you are standing properly.
- Under no circumstances walk around with your hands in your pockets.

Facial expression

The perfect gentleman would never let his views show on his face. It is very important that your face does not reflect your mood or betray your thoughts. The face, as we know, can be read like an open book, and it is all too easy to let what you are thinking show. Little wonder, then, that we have so many sayings in English to describe facial expressions.

> 'Down in the mouth', 'turn his nose up', 'face like a wet weekend', 'tight-lipped', 'raise your eyebrows', 'roll your eyes', 'grin like a Cheshire cat', 'all ears', 'a knitted brow'.

We all know how to send signals with facial expression and, indeed, it is possible to have whole conversations or even pass secret information without ever saying a word.

and some more hints for keeping your facial expression under control...

- Keep an open face, one that conveys a friendly disposition, a face that is ready to smile.
- Do not let your face show your thoughts, especially if they happen to be negative or discriminatory.
- You must never allow your face to 'say' anything that may be read or misconstrued. You must never show your disapproval or that you are bored.

BE YOUR OWN
VALET

THE VALET

valet *n.* servant who takes care of a man's clothes, etc. before 1400 *valette*, borrowed from Old French *valet*, variant of *vaslet* or man's servant; from Gallo-Romance *vasellittus*, meaning young nobleman, squire, page, diminutive of Medieval Latin *vassallus* from *vassus* servant.

Chambers Dictionary of Etymology, 2004 edition

Not everyone has a butler or a valet. In fact, in reality very few people have a butler or a valet, so most people will have to do their own washing and ironing – and why not? Most married men probably rely on their wives to do the ironing, although I can't see why. Everyone should know how to iron and press their own clothes and, in my opinion, everyone should iron and press their own clothes. Knowing how to look after your clothes and shoes is a vital part of the whole grooming regimen.

How to iron a dress shirt

1. Read the care label in the shirt to confirm the recommended ironing temperatures for the fabric.
2. Set up the ironing board.
3. Fill steam iron with water. If you are using a flat iron, keep a spray bottle of water on hand to dampen the shirt.
4. Plug in the iron and set the correct temperature.

5. When the iron has reached the correct temperature, place the shirt onto the ironing board and iron the collar on the inside, moving from the outside in to avoid creases. Place the cuffs on the board and iron the inside first; as you are doing this, make sure you pull the cuffs straight.

6. Iron the sleeves by placing them onto the board and ensuring that the fabric is pulled taut to avoid creasing the sleeve. When one side is ironed, repeat on the other side.

7. Iron the yoke and shoulders next.

8. Place the side of the shirt on the ironing board and iron the buttoned panel on the inside. Turn the shirt over and iron the panel on the right side, ensuring the seams are ironed well.

9. Iron the back of the shirt to the next panel and repeat the process of ironing the buttoned panel on the inside. Turn the shirt over and iron on the right side.

10. If you are using a steam iron, there is no need to spray the shirt. However, if you are using a flat iron then minimal spraying is required to achieve a creaseless finish.

Hangers

Hang the shirt on a clothes hanger to air. Keep the top button done up to prevent the shirt from falling off the hanger and to maintain the shape of the collar. Hang on a shaped hanger rather than a metal dry-cleaners' hanger to keep the shoulders rounded. Fold the shirt once aired.

How to press trousers

1. Clean tailored trousers every second to third time of wearing. Casual cotton trousers can be washed more frequently. Brush trousers in between cleanings.
2. Read the care label in the garment to confirm the recommended ironing temperatures for the fabric.
3. Set up ironing board and fill the iron only with de-ionised water. Have a spray bottle and a press cloth ready (see step 7, below).
4. Plug in the iron and set the correct temperature for the garment.
5. Lay the trousers on the ironing board flat so that one leg is lying on the other.
6. Press one leg at a time by folding one leg up and out of the way. Pressing one leg on top of the other may seem quicker but you will not get a perfect crease and you will get 'iron shine'.
7. Use a press cloth to eliminate 'iron shine'; this is a piece of cotton cloth that can be dampened and used to form a barrier between the iron and the trousers.
8. Lay the press cloth over a portion of the trouser leg. Place the iron on the cloth and move it to iron the trouser area beneath the cloth using some pressure. When you do this, steam will rise, which means that your trousers are getting a firm crease. Be sure that you have not bunched up any cloth at this point by looking under the trouser leg. Then continue down the legs using the same method, moving onto the other parts of the trousers.

Hanging trousers

Use hangers specially made for trousers and hang them with empty pockets and no belt.

To hang them, keep the trousers together with the creases in line and hang them from the bottom (shoe end), never from the waistband. The best hanger for this is wooden, double-barred, cloth or velvet-lined and like a vice in that it clamps the trousers together. This type of hanger is good because it lets the trousers hang without any chance of hanger creases forming.

Do not hang trousers over the bar of a jacket hanger for any length of time. This forms a hanger crease at the knees, which causes more wear at an already heavily worn area.

If you hang two pairs on a hanger, distribute them across the bar and hang them in opposite directions.

Care of jackets

Protecting a valuable piece of clothing such as a jacket takes some doing! Here are some very useful tricks:

- Jackets, sports coats, blazers and similar items usually only need dry cleaning twice a season.
- Brush the jacket between outings. Unbutton the jacket. Check the pockets and empty them before turning them inside out and brushing them out. Brush the jacket using strong, sweeping motions. Take short, quick strokes, first up against the nap then down with the grain of the fabric.
- Press on the right side of the garment with a damp press cloth and a medium-to-hot iron. The heat is good because, combined with the dampness of the cloth, it produces steam that opens up the fibres of the fabric and eases out the creases. Whatever you do, keep the iron moving; don't press down on the collar and avoid pressing on top of vents, which will cause a shiny outline of the fabric underneath to show.
- If you are short on time, instead of pressing, hang the jacket in the steam that has built up after running a hot shower for about 5–10 minutes. Let the steam build up then turn the shower off before hanging the jacket in the shower cubicle. Unless the jacket has

seriously deep creases, this quick fix can achieve a finish almost as good if not quite the same as pressing. Take the jacket out of the steaming environment and allow it to air thoroughly on a shaped hanger before wearing.

- Don't store jackets in plastic bags, as they do not allow the fabric to 'breathe'. Store them in cloth bags and allow at least 25cm (1in) between each hanger in the wardrobe.
- If the jacket is wet (if you get caught in the rain, for example) dry away from direct heat, which can make the fibres brittle. Hang on a contoured hanger to retain the shape.
- For serious stains, take the garment to a professional dry cleaner to remove them.
- Cold storage is best for wool jackets during the summer and, if at all possible, you should store them clean. Moths find the slightest stain irresistible! Use a natural odourless moth repellent.

Hanging jackets

Always hang the jacket on a contoured hanger with buttons unbuttoned and with nothing in the pockets. Allow the jacket at least 24 hours' rest before wearing again; this will significantly lengthen the life of the garment.

Accessories

Belts

If they are fabric, use a reputable spot cleaner and follow the care instructions.

Minor nicks and scratches in leather belts, which come with everyday wear, can be smoothed out with the correctly coloured shoe polish. For all tanned leathers, minor blemishes can be buffed out with a soft cloth.

Gloves

Leather gloves can be cared for as outlined above for leather belts.

If the gloves are wool (with leather) wash only if you really need to and then in cold water with very mild soap. Rinse and dry flat away from heat. Saddle soap will revive the leather parts.

Neckties

You cannot ignore the fact that, due to the way it is made and the fact that it is tied in a knot every time you wear it, your tie is actually the most perishable item in your wardrobe. The following notes will help to ensure your ties stay like new:

- Serious stains can be removed with spot remover or other mild cleaning agents. Test a small inconspicuous area, such as the back of the tie, first to make sure the remover won't damage the material.

- Do not rub stains, as this causes fabric abrasion and loss of colour. Blot the area instead.
- Do not wash a tie. Most ties will shrink unevenly when washed in water due to different shrink rates of the various materials inside the tie.
- Steam ties to rid them of creases; hold them in the steam of a boiling kettle (careful not to burn your fingers!), but do not let the tie get wet. Avoid ironing ties, as this will flatten the natural edge roll and leave a shine. If you must iron a tie, do so with a cool iron and place a slightly damp pressing cloth between the tie and the iron.
- Knitted ties may be hand washed in lukewarm water with a mild detergent. If you have nothing else to hand, shampoo is very good (this is also true for washing high-quality pullovers). Dry the tie flat; never hang it up when wet, as the weight of the water could stretch the tie.
- Don't wear the same tie two days in a row as they need time to recover their shape.
- Watch for loose threads and cut them off, as pulling them can ruin a tie.

Storing ties

Always store ties untied. Store all types of ties rolled up to avoid stretching. Rolling up the tie from the narrow end first and leave it for a couple of days to remove wrinkles. If you are not rolling up your ties, hang them on a rack designed for the purpose; ties slip and twist on hangers and may fall off. Knitted ties can stretch on the hanger so should always be rolled up to store. Store ties out of sunlight, which causes fading.

Packing a suitcase

Travelling is a part of everyday life. To guarantee that a suitcase of clothes reaches its destination without creases and ready to wear, follow the butler-style guidelines set out below. It is a good idea to check the baggage allowance with the airline before travelling.

Select a suitable-sized suitcase and vacuum the insides to remove any dust. Use acid-free tissue paper between each layer of clothing to separate already worn clothes from clean clothes, to avoid dirt transference, to help avoid the risk of buttons catching on other garments and to reduce the risk of general creasing. Lay in sufficient sheets of acid-free tissue paper to cover the bottom of the case and lay more between each of the following layers.

Place your trousers in, with the waistband in the case and about half of the length of the trouser leg hanging outside of the case. Lay in another pair of trousers as before, but opposite; do this to avoid an uneven surface. That is to say waistband to waistband and the legs hanging out of the other side of the case. Fold and place in jackets. Hang the tail out of the case, towards you and hanging over the long side of the case. Stuff rolled tissue paper in the top of the jacket arms.

Even out the surface with other items. Underwear, socks, T-shirts and folded shirts (with the top, middle and bottom buttons only fastened and tissue paper stuffed into collar area) can be added at this stage. Roll a belt and wrap it in tissue paper or wrap the buckle only and snake it around the sides of the case. Individually wrap ties in tissue paper and lay across the other clothes.

Fold in the trouser ends, one side over the other, and fold in the jacket tail. Place shoes in shoe bags, one at each bottom corner of the case. By packing trousers and jackets in this way you will avoid any serious flat fold creases. Wrap your sponge bag in a couple of plastic bags just in case anything leaks in transit. Place the sponge bag at the bottom of the case.

Unpacking
Unpack with as much care as when packing; keep the tissue paper for the return journey. Place items in wardrobes and on hangers by type, with all T-shirts in one pile and dress shirts either on hangers or in another pile, possibly by colour. Trousers should be put on hangers as soon as possible.

Clothing storage

If you are working in a climate with more than one
season, you should store off-season clothing carefully
to avoid unnecessary damage from insects, mould and
mildew. Wash and dry all garments before storing. Do
not store garments in plastic bags or airtight containers,
as air must be allowed to circulate around the clothes and
allow them to breathe. Storage areas should be dark and
clean; sunlight fades colours and attracts some insects.

and some more hints for optimum clothing storage...

- Leather and suede should be stored in a cupboard
  that is cool and well ventilated. The garments should
  be covered in clean muslin. Softer leather or suede
  garments should be laid flat and padded with
  acid-free tissue paper.
- Always clean clothes before storing; insects are
  attracted to perspiration, spilled food and drink.
- Linen garments should be rolled to avoid permanent
  creasing. Cover with clean muslin.
- Never store clothes in a cold basement or cellar,
  or a hot roof or attic. Extreme temperatures will
  damage clothing.
- Never use a fabric finish or a starch with clothes
  that are to be stored.

- Wool should be thoroughly cleaned, padded and wrapped in acid-free tissue paper. Wool, cotton, silk and linen are all natural fibres, so always store in a well-ventilated area. Knitted and silk items should always be stored flat, wrapped and inter-spaced with acid free tissue paper.
- Store jackets on padded hangers in clean muslin bags.
- Add moth-repellent products to the storage areas.
- It can help to use a chemical product, such as calcium chloride and silica gel, to absorb moisture and prevent mildew. Do not let the product touch the clothing.
- Do not dry clean garments then store them. It has been suggested that the chemical residue left in the fabric after cleaning will damage the fabric and possibly compromise stitching. Dry clean an item just prior to wearing.
- Protect clothing from wood acids by lining drawers with an acid-free shelf paper. Never use leftover wallpaper or gummed backed papers; the backings are a feast for moths.

Removing stains from clothing

Removal of difficult stains is nearly always a job for the professional, but there are a few basic rules to follow if you attempt the cleaning yourself.

Red wine

Pouring white wine on the affected area seems to thin the red stain out, but the old wives' tale of pouring salt on the area is not beneficial; the salt reacts with the tannins in the wine and sets the stain fast. If the wine is on a carpet mop up as much as possible and use a good carpet cleaner immediately. Dab at the stain, don't rub it around as this only spreads it. Wash a garment in the normal way before the area dries.

White wine

White wine is easier to remove than red wine and doesn't stain so much; rinse the area and then wash in the normal way. Treat carpet stains as per red wine, above.

Tea and coffee

A fresh tea or coffee stain will respond to soaking in a hand-hot washing product solution followed by rinsing. If the stain is set and the fabric suitable, soak and then wash at a high temperature.

Curry

Wash off as soon as possible with a washing powder that contains bleach. A small stain can be soaked in a stain-remover solution before washing.

Butter or margarine

Scrape off as much of the fat as possible. Pre-treat with a liquid detergent. If the fabric is suitable, wash at a high temperature. If not, treat with a solvent then air, or rinse and wash according to the fabric care label.

Milk or cream

Soak in a warm washing solution using a biological washing product and then wash according to the fabric.

Anti-perspirant and deodorant

Apply a liquid detergent then, if the fabric is suitable (check the label), soak in a warm washing solution using a biological washing product.

Shoe polish

Pre-treat with a liquid detergent then, if the fabric is suitable (check the label), wash at a high temperature.

Flower pollen

You can try to lift off the pollen with something like gaffer tape, but never use water on furniture coverings. Use a stain remover on garments and wash in the normal way.

Unidentified stains

When a garment is found to be stained and the cause is unknown it is usually best to take it to a dry cleaner or laundry that can perform the stain removal. However, if the garment is washable, you could try rinsing in cold water followed by normal washing.

Care labels

There is no shortage of guidance for anyone wanting advice on how to care for fabrics or garments. It can be found in newspapers, magazines, manufacturer's leaflets, washing machine instruction manuals and on washing product packs.

You would have to be a qualified textile engineer to determine the appropriate care of a garment simply by looking at it. Even knowing the fibre content is not enough since so many dyes and finishes are applied. Care labels are therefore required by law to help consumers.

The label describes the minimum recommended safe care. For example, on 'washings' your care label should tell you the correct method required (machine or hand), the safe water temperature, the safe drying temperature and the safe ironing temperature. If bleach is needed and chlorine bleach is not safe, the label should warn against it.

When the label says, 'wash or dry clean, any normal method', it means the product can be: machine washed at any temperature; ironed, even hot, if ironing is needed; bleached with any type of bleach; dry cleaned in any common solvent.

But such a simple label is very rarely used. Most care labels provide more detailed information. Manufacturers may voluntarily go further than the minimum required, protecting certain features of the garment or advertising the advantages of the fabrics.

Manufacturers who take the trouble to put care labels in their garments do so because they are proud of the things they produce and want the purchaser to get the best from them. For example, the label 'dry clean only' or 'professionally dry clean' means just that – the garment has to go to a dry cleaner. However, if an item can't be dry cleaned the label should warn you.

Care instructions can be found sewn into the garment, at the neck or in a side seam. Sewn-in labels are the most satisfactory because they last the life of the garment. Swing labels are also used but are not helpful because they get taken off and more often than not discarded.

If at any time you commence cleaning without reading the label you are taking a hefty risk!

How to sew on a button

Washing, ironing and constantly opening and closing your shirt buttons puts an enormous strain on the button and it's really only a question of time before it will come off. If you notice the button is loose and likely to come off, try to remove it and keep it rather than losing it. Some very expensive shirts may have unique buttons and may be hard to replace. If you are away on a business trip, wearing an alternative shirt at a moment's notice may not be an option and you may not have access to a sewing service such as your dry cleaner to do it for you. Knowing how to sew on a button could be very important and, once you know how to do it, you won't panic if a shirt button comes off just before a meeting or a business dinner. Hotel rooms often provide a sewing kit along with the standard selection of shampoo and shower gel, but having a kit with you when you travel can turn out to be very useful. This is what you do:

1. Use a matching button. If you can't find one, there are normally a couple of spares sewn at the bottom of most dress shirts. Failing this, cut the lowest button off from the very bottom of the shirt and use that, because no one will see that it is missing.
2. Select a needle and choose a matching colour thread; if you haven't the exact colour get as close as you can.

3. Trim and cut away the old thread from the lost button site.
4. Cut a piece of new thread about 75cm (2½ft) in length and thread one end through the eye of the needle. Then pull the two ends together and knot them.
5. Place the button on the location of the missing button and hold it in place with one hand. Then, from the underneath, push the threaded needle through the shirt material and through one of the holes in the button. Then push the needle through one of the other holes, back through the shirt and pull the thread tight. Repeat these two steps until all of the holes in the button have been used two or three times each.
6. So that there is a small gap between the shirt and the button, making buttoning easier, bring the needle up through the shirt material from the underneath and do not go through the button but instead wrap the thread a few times around the thread that is in between the shirt and the button.
7. Now push the needle back through the shirt and cut the thread. Leave enough to hold so that you can tie the two ends together to form a knot, then cut off the excess.

If this is all too much for you and you have the time, get the hotel laundry to sew your button on for you!

WATCH YOUR STEP

*I still have my feet on the ground,
I just wear better shoes.*

Oprah Winfrey

BOOTS AND SHOES

Feet are generally overlooked and, unfortunately, the value of clean, well cared for shoes goes largely ignored as well. A clean pair of shoes is a must for the well-dressed gentleman. Shoes say more about the person than is ever realised. Clean and cared-for shoes project attention to detail and pride in the appearance, whereas dirty, scuffed shoes that should be polished give out the exact opposite signals – that you are slovenly or lazy. Couple a smart suit with a filthy pair of shoes and you might just as well wear jeans and a moth-eaten T-shirt, as the effect of the suit will be completely lost.

It has been calculated that the average person spends at least 6,200 hours a year in shoes and half of that time is spent walking. Good-quality shoes are therefore clearly very important.

Wearing the correct shoe with the correct outfit is vital. No one in their right mind would wear trainers with a city suit, for example. The old adage about not wearing brown in town is frankly a bit outdated; some dark brown shoes can look exceptional with a business suit. Most bench-made shoes incorporate a section of cork in the sole, which over time adapts to the shape of your feet, making the whole wearing experience more comfortable. Match them carefully with the outfit: Oxford toe caps with a lounge suit; brogues

(Americans call them wingtips) with a business suit;
and loafers, polished or suede, with chinos. Scuffed suede
shoes, as long as they are not too scuffed, can give a very
casual look. Gentlemen's suede shoes are never worn
exactly box-fresh; a few scuffs are acceptable or at
least they should look a little lived in.

Dress a medium-priced suit with expensive shoes
and the whole picture looks expensive. This is a
system that my grandmother referred to as 'cheap coat,
expensive buttons'. And she would have known, having
been a cutter and fitter of debutantes' gowns on Duke
Street, London in the early 1920s. Take my word for
it, this works.

Make sure you get the right shoe size – too small
and you will be blistered and hobbling in no time, a
disadvantage if you intend to waft around a dance floor
all night; hobbling at a black tie event just would not do.
Too big and you will be drifting around inside the shoes;
a situation that leads to very tired feet and blisters. Your
socks will find their way down and into the shoe as
well! Shoes should feel comfortable the moment you
try them on; don't accept a salesperson's comment
like 'Oh, they'll stretch after a while'. Most people's
feet are different sizes, with the right foot often very
slightly larger than the left. Try the right shoe first
because you will know that the left will fit if the
right is comfortable.

Cleaning leather boots and shoes

Cream polish stage

Follow these steps the first time you clean a new
pair of shoes:

1. Remove debris and dust before you start; a slightly
   damp sponge is good for this or you could carefully
   brush the debris off.
2. Make absolutely sure that the colour of the polish
   you use is right for the shoes. If you don't have the
   exact colour, get some for the next time. Always
   use a lighter tone, never darker.
3. Apply a small amount of cream polish to a soft
   clean cloth.
4. Using a circular motion, rub the cream into the shoe.
   Begin at the toe and work your way around the shoe.
5. Take another clean piece of cloth and lightly buff each
   shoe to a high shine.

Thereafter

Open a tin of solid polish, the correct colour, and
using the 'putting on' brush, dip the brush into the
polish. Carefully work the polish into the shoes using the
brush. Be mindful to work some polish into the welt area
as well – that is the small gap at the junction of the upper

and the sole. Carefully polish the tongue. Finally, turn the shoe over and polish the area underneath that never touches the ground; this part should always be polished. Years ago, the butler polished the laces too – who knows, some may still do it.

Leave the polish on the shoe for as long as you can to allow the polish to be absorbed and to nourish the leather. Finally, brush to a high shine with the brush reserved only for 'taking off'.

Now you can 'spit and polish' the toes if so desired.

Spit and polish

This is a very traditional and important part of the butler's shoe-cleaning regime. With your index finger wrapped in a piece of soft cloth, dip the end into a high-quality polish. Then, after dipping the finger of polish in a saucer's depth of cold water, apply it only to the toes of the shoes with a circular movement. Continue until a deep shine is achieved.

Butlers don't actually spit on the shoes anymore but it is said that the water hardens the polish so that the deep shine can be achieved. Shoes that have been polished in this way a few times take on a fantastic shine.

'La Grande Passion de Pied'

Berluti, a French company, is a bespoke shoe-maker with shops in Paris and London. They have made shoes for individuals since 1895, including Pablo Picasso, Andy Warhol and Robert de Niro.

Olga Berluti, the granddaughter of the company's founder, is passionate about feet and her creations. She started a unique club for the owners of her handmade masterpieces to meet and celebrate their shoes. The first meeting of The Swann Club was held at the Hotel Carillon in Paris in 1992. The club is named after Proust's hero of *À la Recherche du Temps Perdu*, who was also a bit of a dandy. First and foremost the members meet for dinner. Then, before they leave, a bizarre ritual takes place. The members remove the tablecloth and shoe polishes are brought in. Every member takes off their shoes and polishes them using pure Venetian linen wrapped around their fingers and dipped in polish and then Dom Pérignon champagne. Beforehand, the shoes have to be washed and exposed to the light of the moon. 'Actually it has to be the rising quarter moon,' says Berluti. 'The moon gives transparency to the leather, the sun burns and the moon burnishes' and 'the alcohol makes them shine more', she insists.

It's a champagne 'spit and polish' really; it's just the lunar cycle part I'm a bit lost with (although Berluti does specify a waxing moon). I tried leaving a pair of my hand-sewn Oxfords out in the moonlight once and they just got damp. "Chaqu'un à son 'shoe'", I suppose.

Cleaning suede shoes

1. Loosen dirt by gently rubbing the surface with a suede brush.
2. Using short, quick strokes, lift the nap and remove the dirt. Brush in the direction of the nap.
3. To revive tired suede, hold the shoe for a few moments in the steam of a boiling kettle but do not allow them to get soaking wet from the steam. Allow them to dry then give them a gentle brushing.
4. If suede shoes get wet, stuff them with newspaper. As they dry, the paper will help to keep their shape.

Cleaning fabric shoes

1. Spot clean with warm water, detergent and a soft brush.
2. Rinse with water.
3. Pat with a soft cloth or towel to remove excess moisture.
4. Air dry.
5. Some trainers seem to come out well from the washing machine in a pillow case on a low heat.

Care of riding boots

Riding boots are apt to pick up grease and sweat from
the horse as well as mud and grit, so need special care.
Every now and then leather boots should be cleaned
with a commercial boot cleaner or white vinegar.
Commercial leather cleaners should be all natural
because silicone-based products sit on top of the
leather and do not allow the material to 'breathe'.

1. Wipe the boots with a slightly damp cloth. If the dirt
   build-up is considerable, remove as much as possible
   while still soft. Let the boots air dry completely.
2. Dab on leather cleaner with a soft cloth and allow
   it to soak in.
3. Scrub each boot with the soft cloth and allow to
   dry overnight.
4. Once dry, you can polish the boots in the same
   way as you would shoes, using a good wax product.
5. Apply talcum powder to the inside leather lining.
6. Store polished riding boots in specially shaped
   boot trees.

Look after suede riding boots as you would suede shoes
(see page 127). Some suede can be sprayed for extra
weather and dirt proofing.

Soaking-wet riding boots
Stuff the insides with newspaper or paper towels and air
dry normally. Under no circumstances dry your riding
boots on a radiator, because they are prone to cracking
if dried too quickly on artificial heat.

and some more hints for keeping shoes in good condition...

- When shoes that are normally polished are new, clean them with a cream polish for the first time. Cream polish contains lanolin, which is an oily, waxy material derived from wool. It is ideal to give shoes the coating they need to condition the leather.
- Brush shoes with a natural hair brush, such as horsehair, since synthetic brushes tend to be wiry and hard and can scratch the leather.
- Rotate a shoe wardrobe. Wearing the same shoes day in, day out doesn't give the leather a chance to 'breathe' properly.
- Always use a shoe horn when you put on a shoe, especially when you put a hand-sewn shoe on for the first time.
- Store shoes in shoe trees and have lighter-weight shoe trees for travelling.
- When travelling, pack the shoes in individual shoe bags to prevent scratching and rubbing on clothing.
- Try shaking some powdered bicarbonate of soda into trainers to get rid of that trainer smell.

Straight laced

No doubt you were taught how to tie your shoe laces a long time ago, but were you shown how to lace them? I've come across many people who can't do this during my various assignments as a butler; mind you I've come across just as many who couldn't boil a kettle either.

Here's just one way to lace a pair of shoes – probably the easiest and the best. This style that would suit evening shoes, an Oxford toe cap and almost all business shoes. It's found on most new shoes, and is the shoemaker's factory setting.

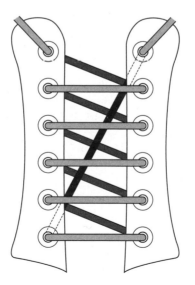

Straight lacing, single helix or factory lacing

1. The lace runs straight across the bottom. The ends of the laces are fed into both eyelets.
2. One end is fed diagonally from the bottom eyelet and out of the top eyelet on the other side.
3. The other end is zigzagged up through the remaining eyelets.

Buy the right length laces; they are normally sold by eyelet count. Get the right colour and style – round laces and flat laces suit different shoes, so don't get them mixed up. If your laces are too long you can always tie a double bow.

The modern gentleman certainly does wear
jewellery and it is true, to a point, that the right
jewellery can make an impressive style statement
on a man. A man should wear the jewellery, it should not
wear the man. Proceed with caution, bearing in mind
that you should not pile it on; just opt for a piece or
two and choose carefully. With men's jewellery the
secret is to stay refined, simple and stylish. Less, in this
case, really is more. I doubt if you would see a city gent
with a diamond stud in his ear, opting for a visible tattoo
or having a tongue stud fitted, but it's all down to
personal taste. Who's to say what is right or wrong?

Some major designers are launching collections just for
men. The men's market seems to be taking off in a big
way and tastes are changing. They are using a lot of
diamonds, so remember the buying and wearing of fine
jewellery comes with this one caveat … the lady in your
life might not be too happy with you wearing pieces
that are better than hers, so it might be an idea to go
shopping together!

Watches

Watches make a statement similar to that made by the
wearing a fine pair of shoes. A watch speaks volumes
about the wearer and, in common with shoes, a good
watch shouts taste and class. Stainless steel, silver or
another silver-coloured metal with a fine leather band
will always look good with a business suit, while gold

is great with evening dress. Wearing an enormous, diamond-encrusted counterfeit Rolex would look ridiculous with a business suit. Similarly, if you have a digital readout watch made of plastic that doubles as a piece of cardiology equipment or a sat-nav, it should stay in your locker after the workout – you should never wear it with your business suit.

Rings

Wearing excessive jewellery on your hands is an absolute no-no. Wear your wedding ring if you have one and want to, but nothing says you must. With rings, it's best to stay discreet and understated. Never wear more than one at a time on one hand. One high-quality piece is infinitely better than a fistful of tat.

Cufflinks

First worn in the 1700s in the form in which we know them today, cufflinks are elegant accessories that give a sparkle to any suit or evening dress.

Shirts with a double cuff still seem to appear the most prestigious. The cuff doesn't have button fastenings, but features buttonholes only. Cufflinks are pushed through the cuff to hold them together. This is a great opportunity to wear some miniature artwork if you are so inclined. In fact, you can trace every significant movement in art history through the design and development of cufflinks. There are literally thousands of designs but the best advice is to stay reasonably sized.

The most expensive cufflinks ever went under the hammer in 1987, when they were sold at auction for approximately £220,000. They were originally a present from Wallis Simpson to soon-to-be King Edward VIII. They consisted of diamonds set in platinum.

Other accessories

As far as chains go you should tread very carefully. Too much yellow gold will look excessive. Chains should be fairly plain and discreet and never, ever worn outside over a shirt and tie. Do this and you will look like Del Boy and you wouldn't want to look like a 'plonker', would you?

Anything other than a medic bracelet or a hospital identification wristband is worth avoiding. Adornments such as threaded shells and tatty, ragged woven or plaited things worn around the wrist might look *de rigueur* and are acceptable on the younger generation, but they are not really the thing for the grown up. However, it is just possible that the odd bangle hidden under the work suit might hint at a wilder side. Identity bracelets bearing your own name (or anyone else's for that matter) are quite definitely verging on the uncouth and are best handed in at the pawnbrokers. If you really must, a tasteful leather bracelet may be acceptable.

Avoid wearing keys on a hook on the belt loop of your trousers, or wearing your mobile phone on the belt like a cowboy's six shooter in a holster.

You can pin or tie your day pass at the races to your suit by all means but avoid badges that display your favourite football team or for that matter your national flag unless you need a constant reminder of your nationality.

Pieces of visible yellow gold in the mouth, especially in the front, are an absolute faux pas. If your dentist suggests it, get up out of the chair and run, because you are definitely in the wrong place. For a thankfully short time in oral cavity fashion history having a diamond cemented into a front tooth was the *dernier cri* in some circles, mainly on Rodeo Drive if I remember rightly. It might look a bit out of place on the Northern Line, not to mention being a very good way of ruining an otherwise perfectly healthy incisor.

DRESS CODES

FORMAL DRESS

The following is a guide to formal dress, and explains exactly what you are expected to wear when you see the terms 'morning dress' and so on, on your invitation.

Morning dress

Morning dress is worn to weddings, funerals and formal horse racing events such as Royal Ascot. The attire may be worn in the afternoon but not to an event that starts after 7pm. Morning dress consists of the following:

- A black or grey single-breasted morning coat. This coat is also known as a 'cutaway' and is equestrian in origin. In the 19th century, men wore a jacket that was essentially a frock coat with the front cut away, which was worn when riding in the morning. This should not be confused with a tailcoat.
- The waistcoat is grey or buff (a sandy colour) or sometimes white.
- Pinstriped or plain grey trousers can be worn, but never with turn-ups.
- A white cotton, silk or linen shirt. Pair a long necktie with a standard collar and double cuffs. Wear a single-cuffed and a winged collar if worn with a cravat (as at weddings).
- Black or grey top hat.
- Black shoes, but without toe caps, brogueing or patterns.
- Black socks.

Traditionally, when worn at weddings, only the bridegroom and the bride's father wear the grey alternative. Grey top hats should only be worn with the grey alternative. Wear a grey top hat to sporting events, weddings and presentations at Court but never wear one in the evening, when riding to hounds or when the Court is in mourning.

Morning suit

A morning suit is slightly less formal than morning dress. It consists of a three-piece, matching mid-grey suit; a morning coat, a waistcoat that can be double- or single-breasted and trousers. A striped shirt with contrasting white collar and cuffs may be worn. This suit can be worn at Ascot and to weddings.

Military dress

Military mess uniform is suitable for most formal events. In the navy 'mess dress' is worn for formal events but you must be entitled to wear it.

Scottish Highland dress

Scottish Highland dress is the Highland version of morning dress. It consists of a black or charcoal coloured Argyll, Braemar or Crail jacket, black or charcoal barathea waistcoat to match the jacket and a kilt or trews (tartan trousers). A white shirt with cufflinks, a tie in a colour to match the kilt, a kilt hose in cream or to match the kilt (not tartan), flashes, sporran, dirk and a *sgian dubh* (a ceremonial dagger) are also worn. Shoes should be black Ghillie brogues.

Evening dress

If an invitation states that evening dress is 'optional', assume that you must or should wear evening dress. That applies the ladies too. The use of the word 'optional' is simply a polite way of telling you to wear evening dress.

White tie
White tie is the correct formal equivalent to morning dress (i.e. evening dress). It is worn at the most glamorous evening parties and very formal evening occasions, such as a state banquet or the state opening of parliament. The outfit consists of a black evening tail coat, also known as a swallow-tail coat, the cut of which is slightly different to that of the morning coat. A tail coat has a horizontal cutaway design, waist length at the front and knee length at the back.

Black dress trousers are worn without turn-ups but with a double braid down the outer seam. A white stiff-fronted shirt is worn, with mother-of-pearl, or gold studs and cufflinks. The bow tie and waistcoat are both white pique, otherwise known as marcella, to match the shirt front. Shoes must be black and may be patent.

Black tie

The Americans refer to black tie as a tuxedo, and why not? After all, it did come about at the Tuxedo Park Club in New York in 1886, when one member, Mr Griswold Lorillard, went to a ball dressed in a short jacket that he had styled on the English 'smoking' jacket. In France and elsewhere the jacket is known as *le smoking*; the shawl collared jacket is known as *le smoking Deauville*; and the peaked-lapel version is *le smoking Capri*.

How to tie a bow tie

1. Cross one end over the front.

2. Take the long end through the centre.

3. Form a loop with the short end.

4. Bring the long end over it.

5. Form a loop with the long end.

6. Push it through the knot behind the front loop. Adjust and tighten.

and some more hints for wearing black tie...

- The first stumbling block is possibly the tie choice. There are three: a pre-tied bow tie, a hand-tied bow tie (see page 143) and a black necktie. Tie the tie yourself if you have time and you are wearing a wing collar or a regular collar. Wear the pre-tied bow tie if you are in a hurry and you are not wearing a wing collar. A pre-tied bow tie cannot be worn with a wing collar because all the mechanical bits will be exposed. Wearing a black necktie is more modern. Dancing late at night with your bow tie untied around an open-necked evening shirt is not the done thing.
- The single-breasted jacket is a classic and fits all shapes. The double-breasted jacket looks good on a taller man but if you are under 1.8m (6ft) tall, stick with the single-breasted option. The shawl collar jacket, the style reminiscent of Sean Connery in the very first Bond movie, is now very outdated. Unless you are going to a retro party, avoid it. Save the white jacket for an evening bash in the Caribbean, as it will look out of place in the city. The smoking jacket is an alternative and is a less formal jacket, usually velvet, with a shawl lapel, which is frogged with loops of silk braid. Black was known to take on a greenish hue in the early days of artificial light, so the midnight blue option was introduced by the then Prince of Wales and remains the only acceptable alternative to black.

- Trousers should be in a black shade that matches the jacket, with a black satin braid down the length of the outside seam.
- Should you opt for wearing one, the biggest mistake is to wear a cummerbund with the pleats facing downwards. Unless you are wearing a Red Sea rig, avoid wearing red all together. Cummerbunds were first worn around 100 years ago when gentlemen did not have pockets in their evening trousers and only carried money in their jackets. The pleats in the cummerbund were used as a place to keep theatre ticket stubs. Because a double-breasted jacket is never worn unbuttoned and the waist never left exposed, a cummerbund should not be worn with such a jacket.
- Wear a white shirt. The cut and collar is an individual choice. Keep it simple and, if the shirt has double cuffs, wear silver, discreet cufflinks.
- Wear your own, highly polished, black leather shoes. Avoid wearing patent leather shoes from the hire shop, which will doubtless leave you unable to walk the next day.
- A point worth remembering is that 'black tie' is designed to showcase women, not men. The cut and colour should not be messed with – sticking with the conventional black and white is the best bet. The ensemble should be seen as a sartorial blank upon which a beautifully groomed and elegant woman can drape herself all evening.

Dress Codes for the English Season

'The Season', as the British social season is known, is not as stiff and formal as it used to be. However, it is still formal enough to offer entertainment value unrivalled anywhere else in the world. Where Her Majesty the Queen has an official role to play, there are dress and behaviour codes that make the events very special; a quintessentially British summer pastime.

As far as dress codes go, the best advice is to adhere to exactly what is stated on your invitation. If you are in any doubt, it's always a good idea to ask. Read the invitation carefully; you don't want to be the only one that turns up dressed as Elvis.

The Chelsea Flower Show

This central London event usually lasts for a week in mid-May. The show is held on the premises of the Royal Hospital, Chelsea, and is hosted by the Royal Horticultural Society (RHS). This gardening show is without doubt the leading horticultural exhibition in the world and tickets are sold out very quickly.

Monday is reserved for the Royal family and the Charity Gala preview in the evening. Tuesdays and Wednesdays are for RHS members only.

Hats and ties are worn by the smarter visitors, but there are no dress-code rules.

Glyndebourne

Originating in 1934, the Glyndebourne Opera festival has come a long way. The old barn was replaced by elegant new opera hall in the 1990s. The beautiful gardens still offer a unique experience, where you can picnic in a unique old-country-house setting. Evening gown and black tie are *de rigueur*. If you are arriving from abroad and do not want to hire a car, there is a special train from London Victoria Station to Lewes in Sussex.

Louis Vuitton Classic

The Louis Vuitton *Concours d'Elegance* of vintage cars normally takes place in early June. One of the newer events of the Season, it is held on the premises of the Hurlingham Club, which owns a beautiful white mansion set in a landscaped garden in West London. The event is by invitation only and tickets for the day are available through Louis Vuitton in London, if you are on their client list. The black-tie dinner is for members of the Hurlingham Club and their guests only.

Epsom Derby

The Epsom Derby, named after its originator Lord Derby, is the original derby upon which all other derby races in the world are modelled. First run in 1780, it is one of England's top horse races, attracting excellent horses and beautifully turned-out visitors. The Derby is run at Epsom, which is about 48km (30 miles) south of London, and is normally held in early June. The Queen attends on the Saturday, which is Derby Day, and is part of the Derby Festival. The elegant crowd get tickets for the Queen's Stand.

In the Queen's Stand on Ladies Day gentlemen are asked to wear a jacket, collar and tie. Hats are not compulsory but many wear them. Jeans and sports shoes are not permitted. In the Queen's Stand on Derby Day gentlemen must wear black or grey morning dress with a top hat, or service dress. Ladies are asked to wear formal day dress or trouser suit with a hat. In the Grandstand on both days dress is smart casual with no jeans or trainers. Most people like to dress up for Ladies Day and Derby Day. In the Grandstand hospitality boxes gentlemen are asked to wear a jacket, collar and tie. Ladies do not have to wear a hat but many do.

Royal Ascot

Top hats, the attendance of the Queen and the best racing mark Royal Ascot, which takes place in mid-June every year from Tuesday to Friday. Thursday is Ladies Day where the ladies appear in the smartest outfits and huge hats. An absolute 'must' of the Season, Royal Ascot featured in the Rodgers and Hammerstein musical *My Fair Lady*. The first race at Ascot, which is close to Windsor Castle, was run in 1711 and the Royal Enclosure, where the royals are to be found during the festival, was introduced by King George IV in 1820, initially for his close friends. The most prestigious place to be is in the Royal Enclosure, if you can get in! Of course, you must have a picnic in car park No. 1. Tickets for the Royal Enclosure are difficult to get but you could try the Ascot Office at St James's Palace or, if you are a foreign national, your country's embassy in London.

In the Royal Enclosure, gentlemen are requested to wear either black or grey morning dress with a top hat. Top hats may not be removed in the Royal Enclosure. Service dress may be worn and overseas visitors may wear the national dress of their country. It is permitted to wear Jodhpur, Chelsea and Oxford boots as an alternative to black shoes with morning dress at Royal Ascot and a flower in the buttonhole. Ladies are required to wear smart day dress, below the knee, with a hat. Trouser suits should be of matching material.

On the grandstand, gentlemen are required to wear a suit or a jacket, in both cases with a tie. Jeans, shorts, sports attire or trainers are not permitted. To avoid any doubts you may have, this includes football and rugby shirts, T-shirts and sweatshirts. Ladies usually dress smartly for this occasion. Many ladies wear hats although it is not obligatory.

Box holders who are also Royal Enclosure badge-holders should follow the Royal Enclosure dress code. Box holders who are not Royal Enclosure badge-holders are required to wear morning dress or a suit or jacket, in both cases with a tie. The majority of ladies wear hats although this is not obligatory. Jeans, shorts, trainers or sports attire are not permitted.

No formal dress code applies in the Silver Ring. However, going without a shirt altogether is not permitted at any time.

Wimbledon Lawn Tennis

Wimbledon in late June and early July is one of the pillars of the summer season, with strawberries and cream, sunny weather (sometimes), and mainly outdoor lawn tennis. The first official tennis tournament was played in 1877 at the famous 'All England Tennis and Croquet Club', which still organises the event. Wimbledon enjoys Royal patronage and the Duke of Kent is President of the club. The Duchess of Kent generally presents the prizes to the winners of the ladies' and gentlemen's singles and doubles matches. The centre court is where the most important matches are played and the place to be, if you can get tickets. However, it is also good to go out to one of the other smaller courts to soak up the atmosphere.

Dress code for players is all white. There is no dress code for visitors as such, except in the Member's Enclosure, where a jacket and tie is appropriate for members and their guests. Trouser suits are acceptable for the Ladies. No jeans or shorts.

Henley Royal Regatta

Henley Royal Regatta usually takes place in early July. This international event was first held in 1839. In 1851 Prince Albert, Consort to Queen Victoria, became the Regatta's first royal patron. Ever since then, the reigning monarch has always consented to become patron of the boat races in Henley-on-Thames, which is an hour's drive from London. The place to be is in the various enclosures, where socialising seems to be as important as watching the boats.

For those attending the regatta in the Stewards' Enclosure; gentlemen are required to wear lounge suits, or jackets or blazers with flannels and a tie or cravat. Ladies are required to wear dresses or suits with the hemline below the knee and will not be admitted wearing divided skirts, culottes or trousers of any kind. Ladies are also encouraged to wear hats. No one will be admitted to the Stewards' Enclosure wearing shorts or jeans.

'Glorious' Goodwood

A firm fixture in the English summer season for the last 200 years, the famous July races – described by King Edward VII as 'a garden party with racing tacked on' – are world famous. Taking place at what is often described as 'the world's most beautiful racecourse', the five-day festival meeting is a riot of colour, fashion, famous faces and spectacular hats. It's a sensational horse-racing event on top of the Sussex Downs.

In the Richmond enclosure, ladies are encouraged to wear hats for the festival meeting. Gentlemen are required to wear jackets and ties, cravats or polo neck sweaters. Linen suits and the archetypal 'Goodwood' Panama hat are traditionally worn by gentlemen as characterised by Edward VII in the early 20th century.

In other enclosures dress is informal, but going without a shirt altogether is not permitted at any time. Due to the terrain at Goodwood and areas of decking, stiletto heels for women are not recommended. Jeans and shorts are not permitted at any meeting.

Cartier International Polo

The Cartier International Polo Day takes place each
year at the end of July on Smith's Lawn within the Great
Park at Windsor. It is hosted by the Guard's Polo Club.
Founded in 1955, Prince Philip, the Duke of Edinburgh,
has been its President ever since. The Great Marquee is
the place to see celebrities or watch the chukkas from
the grandstand. The Queen is usually present and awards
the prizes, and on occasion the Prince of Wales or his
sons can be seen playing polo.

The dress code here is smart casual in all areas, no
jeans, trainers or sportswear. To get into the restaurant
gentlemen should have collared shirts and jackets – no
shorts are allowed. This is an outdoor event and the
seating is not covered, it is expected that visitors
dress appropriately for the weather.

Cowes Week

The Cowes Week regatta is held for a week at the
beginning of August. The regatta takes place at Cowes
on the Isle of Wight off England's south coast. Cowes
Combined Clubs run the regatta, which is an association
of the famous Royal Yacht Squadron (Britain's premier
sailing club), the Royal London Yacht Club, the Royal
Corinthian Yacht Club and other clubs based in Cowes.
Cowes Week originated in the early 1800s under King
George IV and with its many traditions has been part of
the British summer social season for many years. Cowes
Week is not just for racing; there is also a comprehensive

social scene from parties to balls. There are finale
fireworks on the Friday evening ahead of the close
of the regatta on the Saturday.

During the course of the week the various clubs each
hosts cocktail parties and balls. A lounge suit is expected
at the cocktail parties and black tie at the balls, or mess
dress which is worn by club members. Entry to these
clubs during the day is less formal, with smart sailing
gear acceptable (with the exception of the Royal Yacht
Squadron which demands a more formal dress code all
the time).

Last Night of the Proms
Attended by music enthusiasts from all over the
world, the BBC Henry Wood Promenade Concert
season runs from the middle of July to the second week
in September when the famous Last Night takes place.
The Royal Albert Hall in Kensington in central London is
the venue. Traditionally, the Last Night of the Proms was
the night the establishment returned to London after the
summer break at their country retreats. Try to get a box,
as this is where you can dress up. The Proms were
founded by Henry Wood in 1895, originally for those
people who had to stay in London for the summer and
to promote new music. The BBC has broadcast from the
Proms since 1927.

There is no dress code at the proms. In the words of the
BBC, 'just come as you are!'

On the Links

It would seem to me that nowhere else is dress code so desperately important as at the golf and country club. With most sports, the outfit is designed to be performance-enhancing but, with golf, all you really need are clothes that do not restrict your swinging a club and some comfortable shoes.

However, over the years some very clear guidelines have evolved and, if you expect to be allowed onto the first tee, it is best to stick to the rules. These can differ slightly from club to club and indeed from country to country but if you follow these guidelines you won't go far wrong. Golfers can be seen wearing some fairly colourful get ups, but dressing up to parody some of the more flamboyant players on the professional circuit may lead to criticism. It is expected that your outfit does not distract play or the concentration of others, or give rise to the amusement of others.

The Royal and Ancient Golf Club of St Andrews (R&A) is the governing authority for the rules of golf and the rules of amateur status, within which ideal etiquette is described. However, clothing worn on the course is a matter for individual clubs, and it is entirely up to them to decide what dress code, if any, is to apply; The R&A has no jurisdiction over such matters.

and some more hints for the golf course...

- Wear a golf shirt with a collar and always tuck it in. A polo shirt is ideal.
- Shorts are acceptable but they must be designed for golf, tailored and no shorter than just above the knees. Anything cut off, made of denim or incorporating cargo pockets is not appropriate.
- If you are wearing long trousers, the socks should match the trouser colour. Trousers and shorts should have belt loops but need not have turn ups as these tend to collect bits of grass and sand. Wear a belt.
- In cooler or wet weather wear pullovers and, if need be, specially designed wet weather clothes. Every golf bag incorporates a fixing for an umbrella and it is generally a good idea to have one with you.
- Hats are acceptable but do not wear a baseball cap with the peak facing your back.
- Golf shoes are a must and most clubs now insist that shoes are fitted only with soft spikes. Some clubs do not like it if you change your shoes at the back of your car.
- Wear sunglasses and a sun cream with a high SPF, if you wish.
- If in doubt about the dress code, ask. There maybe a different dress code for the clubhouse and clubhouse events.
- Having mobile phone with you and switched on while playing golf is a big no-no.

APPENDIX

Clothing Sizes

Men's Suits, Coats and Pullovers

UK	32	34	36	38	40	42	44	46
Europe	42	44	46	48	50	52	54	56
United States	32	34	36	38	40	42	44	46

Men's Shirts

UK	14	14½	15	15½	16	16½	17	17½
Europe	35	36/37	38	39/40	41	42/43	44	45
United States	14	14½	15	15½	16	16½	17	17½

Men's Shoes

UK		7	8	9	10	10½	12	13
Europe		40/41	42	42/43	43/44	45	47	48
United States		7	8	9	10	11	12	13

Men's socks

UK			9½	10	10½	11	11½	12
Europe			39	40	41	42	43	44
United States			9½	10	10½	11	11½	12

Hat sizes

UK	6.5	6.625	6.75	6.875	7	7.125	7.25	7.375
Europe	53	54	55	56	57	58	59	60
United States	6.5	6.625	6.75	6.875	7	7.125	7.25	7.375

Sizes many also include the letters S (short), R (regular)
and L (long).

Measuring

a Head: Measure around head staying 2.5cm (1in) above the ear, then refer to chart for nearest size.

b Neck: Measure around the base of the neck. Allow room for wearing comfort.

c Sleeve length: From the centre back of the neck with arm slightly bent, measure around to your wrist bone.

d Chest: Measure around the fullest part under your arms.

e Waist: Measure around the natural waistline, or where you wear your trousers.

f Seat/hip: With feet together, measure around the fullest part of the hip, around 18–20cm (7–8in) below the waist.

g Inseam: Measure an existing pair of trousers from the crotch seam to the hem.

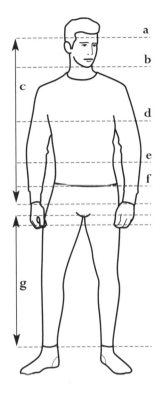

INDEX

accessories 107–108

aftershaves and eau de toilette 45

bathing and showering 29

beachwear 91

body shaving/waxing 51

buttons, how to sew on 117–118

clay masks 69

clothes
care labels 115–116
packing a suitcase 109–110
pressing trousers 103–104
sizes 158–159
storage 111–112
stain removal 113–114
underwear 91

cufflinks 135

deportment 95

designer stubble 47

dress codes 138–155
formal dress 140–145
golf attire 154–155

dressing your age 93

drying 31

ears, cleaning 32

eyes 67

facial expression 97

facial scrubs 68

fingernails 32

five a day 74–76

hair
alopecia 17–19
colouring your hair 23
dandruff 22
dry hair 21
greasy hair 20
keeping healthy 16–17
Norwood-Hamilton scale 18

hands, washing 30

jackets
care of 105–106
removing your jacket 92

jeans 90

jewellery 134–137

keys 137

lips 68

oral hygiene 55 (*see also* teeth)
tongue cleaning 59

posture 95–97

shaving
cuts 45
electric razors 50
fundamentals 42–45
in-growing hairs 49

shirts 84–85
ironing 101–102
removing your shirt 92
rolling up sleeves 93

shoes
and boots 122–123
fabric, cleaning 127

'Le Grande Passion de Pied' 126
polishing 124–125
riding boots, cleaning 128
suede shoes, cleaning 127
threading laces 130

skin care 64–65

smell 28

suits 80–83

sun care 70–71
bronzing creams 71

sweating
combating 37
excessive 39
why and what is it 36
feet 38

teeth
crown and bridgework, care of 61
brushing 57
dentures, care of 61
flossing 58
mouthwash 59
toothbrushes, electric 60

ties
bow tie 143
how to tie 88–89
tie pins 86–87

washing 20–32

water, drinking plenty of 77